HISTORY OF THE UNITED PANJAB

VOLUME 1

BAKSHISH SINGH NIJJAR

Ex-Director, Punjab State, Archives, Patiala

ATLANTIC

PUBLISHERS & DISTRIBUTORS (P) LTD

ATLANTIC
JBLISHERS & DISTRIBUTORS (P) LTD

7/22, Ansari Road, Darya Ganj, New Del
Tel.: +91-11-4077 5252, 2327 3880
E-mail: orders@atlanticbooks.com
Web: www.atlanticbooks.com

Reprint 2026

Published by Atlantic Publishers & Distributors (P) Ltd.

Printed & bound in India by Atlantic Print Services

FOREWORD

Dr. Bakhshish Singh Nijjar, M.A., Ph. D., has followed his history of *Panjab Under the Sultanate (1000-1526), Panjab Under the Great Mughals (1526-1707)* and *Panjab Under the Later Mughals (1707-1759)* now by his *History of the United Panjab*. It covers a period of almost a century from 1849-1947. Like his earlier works it is well written and authorities for the various statements in the text are almost invariably given. As such it can be easily recommended for reference and even for study to students of history of the Punjab under the British.

As his bibliography demonstrates, he has depended for the History of the United Panjab in the nineteenth century (1849-1934) mostly on official records or works, written by Anglo-Indian writers who were not very sympathetic to the Indian point of view. If this makes this study partial occasionally, it must be acknowledged that records of this type serve a useful purpose. One wishes, however, that Dr. Nijjar had not taken Thorburn as his guide as neither his facts nor his inferences were accepted even by the Government of the Panjab at that time.

Coming to the twentieth century Dr. Nijjar's account is more selective. He gives us all the information about the career of various Lieutenant Governors and Governors who governed the Panjab. He gives a story of the Ghadar Movement to its rapid collapse within a few months. Rather than describes the Martial Law regime in the Panjab, he concentrates on the events at Amritsar. Here, however, he presents General Dyer as a straightforward, truth telling soldier entirely unversed in the way of politicians on the authority of Trevasikis ignoring the findings of the Hunter Committee. But left to himself he rightly calls the Jallianwala Massacre "a calculated piece of inhumanity towards utterly innocent and unarmed men and unparalleled for its ferocity in the history of modern British administration." His account of the Gurdwara reform agitation is very full, covering some fiftynine pages. Again it is largely based on the statements issued by the Shiromani Gurdwara Parbandhak Committee. It is good to find the efforts of the Sikhs for securing their "rights" related in one place.

To one reader however it seems that he has made too much of the Hindu-Sikh, Muslim riots in the Panjab during the years 1924-1932 to which he devotes twentyone pages. Thirtytwo pages have been devoted to the Terrorist Movement (The Babar Akalis) in the twenties.

In the thirties he discusses the Communal Award at large emphasising however the special demands of the Sikhs. This is followed by an account of the Civil Disobedience Movement in the Panjab 1930-1934. Here however he could have laid more emphasis on what happened in the Panjab rather than on events of all India importance.

There is a very valuable chapter as the 'Canalization of the Panjab'. Story of the Panjab States 1849-1947 is told elsewhere covering some eighty pages. Here at times, depending upon the authorities used, Dr. Nijjar seems to be pro-Maharajas and elsewhere favouring the struggle of the people of the states which he describes at length.

Another very valuable feature of the work is the chapter on the Kisan and the Muzara Movement in States from 1935 onwards. The chapter on the Panjab Civil Code gives us information not usually found in historical works. Not being a lawyer himself, it is not surprising that Dr. Nijjar seems sometimes to adopt easily the view of the early Panjab administrators whose word was law which nobody – not even a lawyer – could ever anticipate. He forgets that those apostles of personal rule were apt to go astray. Lord Minto had estimated that in the Canal Colonies alone the Colony Administrators had realized in six years twenty lakhs from the cultivators by way of fines which they had no right to extract.

Dr. Nijjar traces the history of the demands of the Sikhs from separate representation with weightage – as the Muslims had got – to 'Khalistan Scheme' when a section of the Sikhs demanded three independent Sikh States, one from Jamuna to Jamrood, second, Nander State in Hyderabad, third, Patna State, he has described the Khaksar movement as well stressing the danger they represented to the peace of the Panjab. His description of the partition of the country and emergence of Pakistan touches the conditions in the Panjab as well. It is interesting to find that though he describes both the Sikh and Muslim preparation for a violent struggle early in 1947, he had not a word to say, probably roughly, about the alleged part that the Jan Sangh is said to have played at this time.

He brings his story to an end by citing a declaration of Master Tara Singh, on 4th March 1947 at Lahore "The time has come when the might of sword alone shall rule. One hundred years from today our yellow flags were flying on the fort of Lahore, the same flag shall fly again."

We recommend the study of this work to all interested in the history of the Panjab. They are likely to find that at places it adds to their knowledge, at other it refreshes the memory of those who lived through these strenuous times. In the end we must congratulate Dr. Nijjar for his laborious task in writing a detailed account of the British Panjab, not hitherto available in one place anywhere else.

SHRI RAM SHARMA

PREFACE

The book is primarily designed to fulfil a long-standing need of the Degree and the Post-graduate students of the Panjab History on the period from 1849-1947. They have always felt greatly handicapped for want of proper and comprehensive material put with a detached objectivity so essential for a historian. Keeping in view the dire need of the students and the teachers, this book has been brought out after many years of research. Almost all the contemporary sources have been consulted to make the book authentic.

This is for the first time that this period has been explored in detail and systematically. Emphasis has been laid to touch every aspect of this period. This book is divided into XIX chapters. The main contents of this work can be summarised as below :

Geography of the Panjab, Panjab at the advent of Britishers, Panjab Under Lawrences, Political history of the Panjab from 1849-1947, North-West Frontier and the British Government, Religious and Political Movements *e.g.* the Kukas, the Komagata Maru, Jallianwala Bagh, Nankana Holocaust, the Jaito Morcha, Guru-Ka-Bagh, Panja Sahib, and Babar Akalis, Riasti Parja Mandal, the Khaksars, Agrarian Agitations, the Legislation, the Civil Administration, Social and Economic life of the Panjab from time to time, the Singh Sabha, S.G.P.C., the revolutionaries of the Panjab, various riots, Canalisation of the Panjab, the Panjab States with the role of their rulers in the Panjab History, Muzara Movements, the Panjab Civil Code, the provincial autonomy, the Unionist-Ministry, and Partition of the Panjab.

Being a detailed study, it has become voluminous. Therefore, it has been thought proper to publish it in three Volumes. The author will welcome suggestions for further improvement of the work.

BAKHSHISH SINGH NIJJAR

CONTENTS

1

Geography of the Panjab

Areas and Boundaries

A geography of the Panjab will embrace an account also of the North West Frontier Province, which in 1901 was severed from it. The Panjab formed into a separate administration, of the small area placed directly under the government of India on the transfer of the capital from Calcutta to Delhi, and of the native states in political dependence on the Panjab Government. It will also be convenient to include Kashmir and the tribal territory beyond the frontier of British India which was politically controlled from Peshawar. The whole tract covered ten degrees of latitude and eleven of longitude. The farthest point of the Kashmir frontier was in 37°2′ N. In the south-east the Panjab ended at 27°4′ N. Kashmir stretched eastwards to longitude 80°3′ and the western most part of Waziristan[1] was in 69°2′ E.

Distribution of Area

The area of the British Panjab was roughly 253,000 square miles. This was two-thirteenth of the area of the Indian British Empire. The area consists of :

		Sq. miles.
(1)	The Panjab	97,000
(2)	Native States dependent on Panjab Government	36,500
(3)	Kashmir	81,000
(4)	North-West Frontier Province	13,000

1. A Political Agency, North-West Frontier Province lying between 32°, 45′ and 33° 15′ N and 69° 30′ and 70° 40′ E with an area of about 21,310 square miles.

(5) Tribal territory under the political control of the Chief Commissioner of North-West Frontier Province roughly. 25,500

Approximately, 1,36,000 square miles was classed as highlands and 1,17,000 as plains. It was distributed as follows over the above divisions :

	Highlands *Sq. Miles*	Plains *Sq. miles*
(1) Panjab, British	11,000	86,000
(2) Panjab, Native States	12,000	24,500
(3) North-West Frontier Province	6,500	6,500
(4) Kashmir	81,000	—
(5) Tribal Territory.	25,500	—

On the north of highlands include the Himalayan and sub-Himalayan Shivalik tracts to the south and east of the Indus, and north of that river the Muztagh-Kara-Koram range and the bleak salt plateau beyond that range reaching almost up to the Kuenlun mountains. To the west of the Indus they include those spurs of the Hindu-Koh which ran into Chitral and Dir, the Buner and Swat[1] hills, the Safed-Koh, the Waziristan hills, the Sulaiman range, and the low hills in the trans-Indus districts of the North West Frontier Province.

Boundary with China

There was a point to the north of Hunza[2] in Kashmir where three great mountain chains, the Muztagh from the south-east, the Hindu-Koh from the south-west, and the Sarikol[3] from the north-east, met. It was also the meeting place of the Indian, Chinese, and Russian empires and of Afghanistan. Westwards from this the boundary of Kashmir and Chinese Turkistan ran for 350

1. North-West Frontier Province, Gazetteer, pp. 210-215.
2. Outside Gilgit itself the area is held by a congeries of petty tribal republics and chieftaincies of which Hunza is the most important ; Schomberg gives them all (except Hunza and Yasin) a bad name for turbulence ; murder, intrigue, avarice, dishonesty, laziness, stupidity and general backwardness (India and Pakistan Supp. p. 384).
3. An offshoot of the Kuenlun.

miles,[1] through a desolate upland lying well to the north of the Muztagh-Kara-Koram range. Finally, in the north-east corner of Kashmir the frontier impinged on the great Central Asia is of the Kuenlun. From this point it turned southwards and separated Chinese Tibet from the salt Lingzi Thang[2] plains and the Indus valley in Kashmir, and the eastern part of the native state of Bashahr, which physically formed a portion of Tibet.

Boundary with United Provinces

The south-east corner of Bashahr was a little to the north of the great Kedarnath[3] peak in the Central Himalaya and the source of the Jamna. Here the frontier struck to the west dividing Bashahr from Teri Garhwal, a native state under the control of the Government of the United Provinces. Turning again to the south it runs to the junction of the Tons[4] and Jamna, separating Teri Garhwal from Sirmur[5] and some of the smaller Simla Hill States. Henceforth the Jamna was with small exceptions the boundary between the Panjab and the United Provinces.

Boundary with Afghanistan

The Frontier ran west and south-west along the Hindu-Koh to the Dorah pass dividing Chitral from the Afghan province of Wakna, and the streams which drained into the Indus from the head waters of the Oxus. At the Dorah pass it turned sharply to the south, following a great spur which parted the valley of the Chitral river[6] from that of its Afghan affulent, the Bashgol. Below the junction of the two streams at Arnawai the Chitral changes its name and becomes the Kunar.[7] Near this point the "Durand" line begins. In 1893 an agreement was made between

1. Omitting curves.
2. Situated to the north of Muztagh Range.
3. West of Vishnuganga, rises another group of peaks above Gangotri, Himat ...Kedarnath, 6,940 metres.
4. Jamna rises in the Kumaon Himalaya, and where it first meets the frontier of the Simla Hill States, receives from the north a large tributary called the Tons.
5. Sirmur, (Nahan) lies to the north of Ambala.
6. British.
7. Kunar river falls into the Kabul river near Jalalabad.

the Amir Abdur Rahman and Sir Mortimer Durand as representative of the British Government determining the frontier line from Chandak in the valley of the Kunar,[1] to the Iranian border. Asmar was an Afghan village on the left bank of Kunar to the south of Arnawai. In 1894 the line was demarcated along the eastern water-shed of the Kunar valley to Nawakotal on the confines of Bajaur[2] and the country of the Mohmands.[3]

Thence the frontier, which had not been demarcated passed through the heart of the Mohmand country to the Kabul river and beyond it to the British frontier post in the Khaibar at Landikhana.[4]

From that point the line, ran on in a south-westerly direction to the Safed-Koh, and then struck west along it to the Sikram mountain near the Paiwar Kotal at the head of the Kurram valley. From Sikram the frontier ran south and south-east crossing the upper waters of the Kurram, and dividing the possessions from the Afghan province of Khost. This line was demarcated in 1894.

At the south of the Kurram valley the frontier swept round to the west leaving in the British sphere the valley of the Tochi. Turning again to the south it crossed the upper waters of the Tochi and passed round the back of Waziristan by the Shawal valley and the plains about Wana to Domandi on the Gomal river, where Afghanistan, Balochistan, and the North-West Frontier Province converged. The Waziristan boundary was demarcated in 1895.

Political and Administrative Boundaries

The boundary described above defines spheres of influence, and only in the Kurram valley it coincided with that of the districts for whose orderly administration the British were held responsible. The British Government wanted from Wazirs,

1. Twelve miles north of Asmar.
2. Bajaur is a very mountainous tract lying to the north-east of Utman Khel country in the N.W.F.P.
3. A tract north-west of Peshawar district, an area of about 1,200 square miles.
4. A post and fort at the top of Khaibar pass. This fort was taken by Afridis in 1897 A.D.

Afridis, or Mohmands to leave their people at peace ; they had no concern with their quarrels or blood feuds, so long as they lived in their mountains or only left them for the sake of lawful gain. Their administrative boundary, which spoke broadly, they took over from the Sikhs, usually, ran at the foot of the hills. A glance at the map would show that between Peshawar and Kohat[1] the territory of the independent tribes came down almost to the Indus. At that point the hills occupied by the Jowaki[2] section of the Afridi[3] tribe pushed out a great tongue eastwards. The British military frontier road ran through those hills, and they actually paid tribesmen of the Kohat pass for their right of way. Another tongue of tribal territory reached right down to the Indus, and almost severed the Peshawar and Hazara Districts. Further north the frontier of Hazara lay well to the east of the Indus.

Frontier with Balochistan

At Domandi the frontier ran to the east, and following the Gomal river to its junction with the Zhob at Kajuri Kach formed the boundary of the two British administrations. Henceforth the general direction of the line was determined by the trend of the Sulaiman range. It ran south to the Vehoa pass, where the country of the Pathans of the North West Frontier Province ended and that of the Hill and Plain Baloches subject to the Panjab Government began. From the Vehoa pass to the Kaha torrent the line was drawn so as to leave Baloch tribes with the Panjab and Pathan tribes with the Balochistan Agency. South of the Kaha[4] the division was between Baloch tribes, the Marris and Bugtis to the west being managed from Quetta, and the Gurchanis

1. A district in the N.W.F.P., which stretched east and west for one hundred miles from Khushatgarh on the Indus to Thal at the mouth of the Kurram valley.
2. The British Government had sent an expedition during the winter in 1877-78. They are the sub-section of the Adam Khel.
3. The Khaibar pass and, the tract lying to the south of it including the Bozar valley and part of Tirah are the home of the six sections of the pass Afridis. Blood fueds.
4. The Mazaris, Burdis Jakrains, and other turbulent tribes inhabited the country between Mithankot and Burdeka (Land ot the Five Rivers and Sindh, Ross, p. 78).

and Mazaris[1], who were largely settled in the plains, being included in Dera Ghazi Khan, the trans-Indus district of the Panjab. At the south-west corner of the Dera Ghazi Khan district the Panjab, Sind and Balochistan met. From that point the short common boundary of the Panjab and Sind ran east to the Indus.

The Southern Boundary

East of the Indus the frontier ran south-east for about fifty miles parting Sind from the Bahawalpur State, till a point was reached where Sind, Rajasthan, and Bahawalpur joined. A little further to the east was the southern extremity of Bahawalpur at 70°8′ E. and 27°5′ N. From that point a line drawn due east could at a distance of 370 miles passed a few miles to the north of the south end of the Gurgaon and a few miles to the south of the border of the Narnaul tract of Patiala. Between Narnaul and the south-east corner of the Bahawalpur state the great Rajasthan desert, mainly occupied in that quarter by Bikaner, thrusted northwards a huge wedge reaching almost up to the Satluj.[2] To the west of the wedge was Bahawalpur and to the east the British district of Hissar. The apex was less than one hundred miles from Lahore, while a line drawn due south from that city to latitude 27.5° north would exceed 270 miles in length. The Jaipur State lay to the south and west of Narnaul, while Gurgaon had across its southern frontiers Alwar and Bharatpur, and near the Jamna the Mathura district of the United Provinces.

THE SIGNIFICANCE OF THE HIMALAYAS IN THE GEOGRAPHY AND HISTORY OF THE PANJAB

The Himalaya

Tibet, which from the point of view of physical geography includes a large and little known area in the Kashmir State to the

1. The vide Indus valley is known as Sindh. The tract between it and the Hills is the Pachadh. It is seamed by hill torrents, three of which, the Vehoa, the Sangarh and the Kaha, have a thread of water in the cold season.
2. Of the five Panjab rivers, the Satluj is the largest and it is the only one that has its source beyond the Indian frontier. Rising from near the Darma Pass on Zanskar range, it joins another branch (Langhchhen Khabah) coming from the east through the Manasarowar and Rakas Lake.

north of the Kara-Koram range, is a lofty, desolate, wind swept plateau with a mean elevation of about 15,000 feet. In the part of it situated to the north of the north-west corner of Nepal lies the Manasarowar Lake, in the neighbourhood of which three great rivers, the Brahmaputra,[1] the Satluj, and the Indus, take their rise. The Indus flows to the north-west for five hundred miles and then turns abruptly to the south to seek its distant home in the Indian Ocean. The Brahamputra has a still longer course of eight hundred miles eastwards before it bends southwards to flow through Assam into the Bay of Bengal. Between the points where these two giant rivers change their direction, there extends for a distance of 1,500 miles the vast congeries of mountain ranges known collectively as the 'Himalayas'.[2] As a matter of convenience the name is sometimes confined to the mountains east of the Indus but geologically the hills of Buner and Swat to the north of Peshawar probably belong to the same system. In Sanskrit literature the Himalaya is also known as 'Himavata', whence the classical Emodus.

The Kumaon Himalaya

The Himalaya may be divided longitudinally into three sections, the eastern or Sikkim, the mid or Kumaon, and the north-western or Ladakh. With the first the British government were not concerned. The Kumaon section lay mainly in the United Provinces, but it included the sources of the Jamna, and contained the chain in the Panjab which was at once the southern watershed of the Satluj and the great divided between the two river systems of Northern India, the Gangetic draining into the Bay of Bengal, and the Indus carrying the enormous discharge of the north-west Himalaya, the Muztagh-Kara-Koram, and the Hindu-Koh ranges into the Indian Ocean. Simla stood on the south-western end of that water-shed, and below it the Himalaya dropped rapidly to the Shivalik foot-hills and to the plains. Jakko, the deodar-clad hill round which so much of the life of summer capital of India revolved, attained a height of 8,000 feet. The highest peak within a radius of twenty-five miles of Simla was the Chor,[3]

1. Also known as Tsangpo.
2. Abode of snow.
3. Chor for the most part a mountain tract, is situated to the north of Giri rising to height of 11,982 feet.

which was over 12,000 feet high, and did not lose its snow cap till May. Hattu, the well-known hill above Narkanda, which was forty miles from Simla by road is 1,000 feet lower. But further west in Bashahr one of the Simla Hill States, Panjab, lying, between 31°6′ and 32°5′ and 77°32′ and 79°4′ E., with an area of 3,820 square miles. (Imperial Gazetteer of India Vol VII, p. 94) the higher peaks ranged from 16,000 to 22,000 feet.

The Inner Himalaya or Zanskar Range

The division of the Himalaya into the three sections named above was convenient for descriptive purposes. But its chief Axis ran through all the sections. East of Nepal it struck into Tibet not very far from the source of the Brahmaputra, was soon pierced by the gorge of the Satluj, and beyond it formed the southern watershed of the huge Indus valley. In the west this great rampart was known as to the Zanskar range. For a short distance it was the boundary between the Panjab and Kashmir, separating two outlying portions of the Kangra district, Lahul and Spiti, from Ladakh. In this section the peaks are from 19,000 to 21,000 feet high, and the Baralacha pass on the road from the Kulu valley in Kangra to Leh, the capital of Ladakh was at an elevation of about 16,500 feet. In Kashmir the Zanskar or Inner Himalayas divided the valley of the Indus from those of the Chenab and Jhelum. It had no mountain to dispute supremacy with Everest,[1] or Kinchinjunga in the Eastern Himalaya, but the inferiority was only relative. The twin peaks called Nun and Kun to the east of Srinagar exceeded 23,000 feet, and in the extreme north-west the grand mountain mass of Naga Parvat[2] towered above the Indus to a height of 26,182 feet. The lowest point in the China was the Zojila[3] (11,300 feet) on the route from Srinagar, the capital of Kashmir, to Leh on the Indus.

The road from Srinagar to Gilgit passed over the Burzil.[4] The Zojila was at the top of the beautiful valley of the Sind river, a

1. World's highest peak 8,848 meters above the sea level.
2. The Pir Panjal takes off from the Great Himalaya range about 100 km south-west of Naga-Parvat and runs 400 km eastwards (The Gazetteer of India—Vol. I. pp. 16-17).
3. The only road to Leh, capital of Ladakh, passes over the Zojila (3,529 m.) an important pass traversing the Great Himalayas.
4. A pass at an elevation of 13,500 feet.

tributary of the Jhelum. The lofty Zanskar range blocked the inward flow of the monsoon, and once the Zojila was crossed the aspect of the country entirely changed. The land of forest glades and green pastures was left behind, and a region of naked and desolate grandeur started.

In all this desolation there are tiny oasis where level soil and a supply of river water permit of cultivation and of some tree growth.

Water divide near Baralacha and Rotang Passes in Kulu

The Indus and its greatest tributary, the Satluj, rise beyond the Himalaya in the Tibetan plateau. The next great water divide was in the neighbourhood of the Baralacha Pass and the Rotang Pass.[1] The route from Simla to Leh ran at a general level of 7,000 to 9,000 feet along or near the Satluj-Jamna watershed to Narkanda (8,100 feet). Here it left the Hindustan-Tibet road and dropped rapidly into the Satluj gorge, where the Luri bridge was only 2,650 feet above sea level. Rising steeply on the other side the Jalauri Pass on the watershed between the Satluj and the Beas was crossed at an elevation of 10,800 feet. A more gradual descent brought the traveller to the Beas at Larji, 3,080 feet above sea level. The route followed the course of the Beas through beautiful Kulu valley to the Rotang Pass,[2] near which the river rises. The upper part of the valley is flanked on the west by the short, but very lofty Bara Bangahal range, dividing Kulu from Kangra and the source of the Beas from that of the Ravi. Beyond the Rotang is Lahul, which is divided by a watershed from Spiti and the torrents which drain into the Satluj. On the western side of this watershed are the sources of the Chandra and Bhaga,[3] which unite to form the river known in the plains.

Mid Himalaya or Pangi Range

The Mid Himalayan or Pangi range, striking west from the Rotang pass and the northern end of the Bara Bangahal chain, passes through the heart of Chamba dividing the valley of the Chenab (Pangi) from that of the Ravi. After entering Kashmir it crosses the

1. 30 miles to the south of it.
2. 13,326 feet.
3. Also called the Chenab.

Chenab near the Kolahoi cone[1] and the head waters of the Jhelum. Thence it continues west over Haramukh,[2] which casts its shadow southwards on the Wular Lake,[3] to the valley of the Kishnganga.[4]

Outer Himalaya or Dhauladhar-Pir Panjal Range

The Outer Himalaya also starts from a point near the Rotang Pass, but some way to the south of the offset of the Mid Himalayan chain. Its main axis runs parrallel to the latter, and under the name of the Dhauladhar[5] formed the boundary of the Chamba State and Kangra, behind whose headquarters at Dharmsala it stood up like a huge wall. It had a mean elevation of 15,030 feet but rose as high as 16,000. It passed from Chamba into Bhadarwah in Kashmir, and crossing the Chenab was carried on as the Pir Panjal range through the south of that State. With an elevation of only 14,000 or 15,000 feet it was a dwarf as compared with the giants of the Inner Himalayan and Muztagh-Kara-Koram chains. But it hid them from the dwellers in the Panjab, and its snowy crest was a very striking picture as seen in the cold weather from the plains of Rawalpindi, Jhelum, and Gujarat. Outer Himalaya continued beyond the gorges of the Jhelum and Kishnganga[6] rivers in the Kajnag and the hills of the Hazara district. Near the eastern extremity of the Dhauladhar section of the Outer Himalaya it sends out southwards between Kulu and Mandi a lower offshoot. This was crossed by the Babbu[7] and Dulchi Passes, connecting Kulu with Kangra through Mandi. Geologically the Kulu-Mandi range appears to be continued to the east of the Beas and across the Satluj over Hattu and the Chor to the hills near Mussoorie,[8] a well-known hill station in the United Provinces. Another

1. 17,900 feet.
2. 16,900 feet.
3. In Srinagar, the summer capital of the State.
4. Probably across it to the mountains which flank the magnificent Kagan glen in Hazara.
5. White ridge.
6. At Domel, in Kashmir, the stage before Kohala the Jhelum receives from the north the waters of the Kishanganga, and lower down it is joined by the Kunhar, which drains the Kagan glen in Hazara.
7. 9,480 feet.
8. The Himachal (the Lesser Himalayan) section of Kumaon comprises mainly two linear ranges, the Mussoorie and the Nag Tibba. The former extends from Mussoorie to Landsdowne, a distance of 120 km.

offshoot at the western end of the Dhauladhar passes through the beautiful hill station of Dalhousie,[1] and sank into the low hills to the east of the Ravi, where it left Chamba and entered the British district of Gurdaspur.

River Valleys and Passes in the Himalaya

While these principal chains can be traced from south-east to north-west over hundred of miles it must be remembered that the Himalaya is a mountain mass from 150 to 200 miles broad, the main axes are linked together by subsidiary cross chains dividing the head quarters of great rivers, and flanked by long and lofty ridges running down at various angles to the gorges of these streams and their tributaries. The typical Himalayan river runs in a gorge with mountains dipping down pretty steeply to its sides. The lower slopes are cultivated, but the land is usually stony and uneven, and as a whole the crops are not of a high class. The open valleys of the Jhelum in Kashmir and of the Beas in Kulu are exceptions. Passes in the Himalaya are not defiles between high cliffs, but cross the crest of a ridge at a point where the chain is locally depressed, and snow melt soonest. In the outer and mid Himalaya the line of perpetual snow is at about 16,000 feet, but for six months of the year the snow-line comes down 5,000 feet lower. In the inner Himalaya and the Muztagh-Kara-Koram, to which the monsoon does not penetrate, the air is so dry that less snow falls and the line is a good deal higher.

Muztagh-Kara-Koram Ranges

The Muztagh-Karakoram mountains form the northern watershed of the Indus. The range consists of more than one main axis. The name Kara-Koram is appropriated to the eastern part of the system which originates at E. longitude 79° near the Pangong lake in the Tibetan plateau, a little beyond the boundary of Kashmir. Beyond the Kara-Koram pass (18,550 ft.) is a lofty upland with salt lakes dotted over its surface. Through this inhospitable region and over the Kara-Koram pass and the Sasser-la (17,500 ft.) the trade route from Yarkand to Leh runs. The road is only open for three months in the year, and the dangers and hardships are great.

1. One of the principal hill stations of the Panjab is situated on the secondary ridge of the Himalayas, on the summit of three mountain peaks east of the river Ravi, 52 miles north of Pathankot.

The Hindu-Koh

The Muztagh chain from the south-east, the Sarikol from the north-east; and the Hindu-Koh from the south-west, meet at a point to the north of Hunza. The last runs westward and south-westward for about 270 miles to the Dorah pass (14,800 feet), separating the valleys which drain into the Indus from the head waters of the Oxus, and, Hunza and Gilgit in Kashmir and Chitral in British India from the Afghan province of Wakhen. The highest point in the main axis, Sad Istragh[1], is in this section. But the finest mountain scenery in the Hindu-Koh is in the great spurs it thrusts out southwards to flank the glens which feed the Gilgit and Chitral to a height of 25,426 feet. From Tibet to the Dorah pass the northern frontier of India is impregnable. It is pierced by one or two difficult trade routes strewn with the bones of pack animals, but no large army has ever marched across it for the invasion of India. West of the Dorah pass the general level of the Hindu-Koh is a good deal lower than that of its eastern section. The vital point in the defences of India in this quarter lies near Charikar to the North of Kabul, where chain thins out, and three practicable passes debouch on the valley of the Kabul river. It is this fact that gives the town of Kabul its great strategic importance.

The highest of the three passes, Hindu-Koh crosses the China at an elevation of 14,340 feet. It is the pass which the armies of Alexander and Babar used. The historical road for the invasion of India on this side had been by Charikar and the valley of the Kabul river to its junction with the Kunar below Jalalabad, thence up the Kunar valley and over one of the practicable passes which connect its eastern watershed with the Panjkora[2] and Swat river valleys, whence the descent on Peshawar is easy.

The Khaibar

A British force advancing on Kabul from Peshawar had never marched by the Kunar and Kabul valley route. It had always taken the Khaibar road, which only followed the Kabul river for less than one-third of the one hundred and seventy miles which

1. 24,171 feet.
2. The Rud, also known as Bajaur, is a tributary of the Panjkora.

separated Peshawar from capital of the Amir. The military road from Peshawar to Landikhana lay far to the south of the river, from which it was shut off by difficult and rugged country held by the Mohmands.

Safed-Koh

From Landikhana the political boundary ran south-west, to the Safed-Koh and was continued westwards along that range to the Paiwar Kotal or pass. The Safed-Koh formed the watershed of the Kabul and Kurram rivers. It was a fine pine clad chain with a general level of 12,000 feet, and its skyline was rarely free fronr snow. It culminated in the west near Paiwar Kotal in Sikaram. To the west of the Peshawar and Kohat districts was a tangle of hills and valleys formed by outlying spurs of the Safed-Koh. This difficult country was in the occupation of Afridis and Orakzais, who were under the political control of the British Government.

The Kurram Valley

The line of advance into Afghanistan through the Kurram valley was easy, and Lord Roberts used it when he marched towards Kabul in 1898. After the war the British Government annexed the valley leaving however the head waters of the Kurram in Afghan territory. The road to Kabul left the river far to the south before it crossed the British frontier at Paiwar Kotal.

Waziristan Hills

Between the Kurram valley and the Gomal river is a large block of very rough mountainous country known as Waziristan from the turbulent clan which occupied it. In the north it is drained by the Tochi. Westwards of the Tochi valley the country rose into lofty mountains. The upper waters of the Tochi and its affluents drained two fine glens known as Birmal and Shawal to the west of the country of the Mahsud[1] Wazirs. The Tochi valley was the direct route from India to Ghazni, and nine centuries ago, when that decayed town was the capital of the powerful kingdom, it must often have heard the tramp of armed men. The loftiest peaks in Waziristan, Shuidar (11,000 feet), and Pirghal (11,600 feet), overhanged Birmal. Further

---

1. Read for details, "*North-West Frontier Province Gazetteer*", pp. 20-25.

south, Wana, the British post in south-west Waziristan, overlooked from its plateau the Gomal valley.

The Gomal Pass as Trade Route

East of the Kajuri Kach, the Gomal river flows through tribal territory to the Gomal pass from which it debouches into the plains of the Dera Ismail Khan district. The Gomal route is the oldest of all trade routes. Down it there yearly pours a succession of Qafilas[1] led and followed up by thousands of well-armed Pathan traders, called Powindahs[2] from the plains of Afghanistan to India. The Powindahs mostly belong to the Chilzai tribes, and were not therefore true Afghans[3]. "Leaving their women and children encamped within British territory on the British border, and their arms in the keeping of the British frontier political officials, the Powindahs make their way southwards with their camel loads of fruit and silk, bales of camel and goat hair or sheep-skin goods, carpets and other merchandise from Kabul and Bokhara, and convey themselves through the length and breadth of the Indian peninsula. They return yearly to the cool summits of the Afghan hills and the open grossy plains, where is countless flocks of sheep and camels are scattered for the summer grazing."[4]

Between Peshawar and the Gomal River

The physical features of the hill country between Peshawar and the Gomal pass may best be described in the words of Sir Thomas Holdich :

---

1. Caravans.
2. The Powindah caravans for the most part enter into the Panjab by the Gomal pass in October, and, passing into this province return in March and April. The principal articles carried are silk, charas, gold and silver thread, and furs from Bokhara, fruits and wool from Ghazni and Qandhahar, madder, wool, 'ghi', tobacco, and asafoetida from Ghazni ; the return trade consisting of indigo, cotton piece-goods, metals, sugar, salt, shoes and leather. The trade, however, did not affect the district of Multan directly, as the Powindahs very seldom unpack any of their wares within it. The district imports piece-goods, hides, salt, and metals, and exports wheat and great millet, the export trade passing down the Indus to Multan, Sukkur, and Karachi. The chief centres of local trade are Dera Ismail Khan, Tank, and Kulachi.
3. They were held to be of Turkish origin.
4. India-Holditch, pp. 80-81.

"Natural landscape beauty, indeed, may here be measured to a certain extent by altitude. The low ranges of sun-scorched, blackened ridge and furrow formation which form the approaches to the higher altitudes of the Afghan upland, and which are almost as regularly laid out by the hand of nature in some parts of the frontier as are the parallels...of the engineer who is besieging a fortress—these are by no means 'things of beauty' and it is this class of formation and this form of barren desolation that is most familiar to frontier officer...Shades of delicate purple and grey will not make up for the absence of the living green of vegetation... But with higher altitudes a cooler climate and snow-fed soil is found, and as soon as vegetation grasps a root-hold, there is the beginning of fine scenery. The upper pine-covered slopes of the Safed Koh are as picturesque as those of the Swiss Alps ; they are crowned by peaks whose wonderful altitudes are frozen beyond the possibility of vegetation, and are usually covered with snow wherever snow can lie. In Waziristan, hidden away in the higher recesses of its great mountains, are many valleys of great natural beauty, where we find the spreading poplar and the inlex in all the robust growth of an indigenous flora... Among the minor valleys Birmal perhaps takes precedence by right of its natural beauty. Here are stretches of park-like scenery where grass-covered slopes are dotted with clumps of deodar and pine and intersected with revulets hidden in banks of fern ; soft green glades open out to view from every turn in the folds of the hills, and above them the silent watch towers of Pirghal and Suidar...look down from their snow-clad heights across the Afghan uplands to the hills beyond Ghazni."[1]

The Sulaiman Range

A well-marked mountain chain runs from the Gomal to the extreme south-west corner of the Dera Ghazi Khan district where the borders of Balochistan, Sind, and the Panjab met. It culminated forty miles south of the Gomal in the fine Kaisargarh mountain, which was a very conspicuous object from the plains of the Derajat. On the side of Kaisargarh there was a shrine called Takht-i-Sulaiman[2] and that was the name by which Englishmen usually knew the mountain, and

1. India—Holdich, pp.81-82.
2. Throne of Solomon.

which had been passed on to the whole range. Proceeding southwards the general elevation of the chain dropped steadily. But Fort Munro[1], the hill station of the Dera Ghazi Khan district, two hundred miles south of the Takht, still stands 6,300 feet above sea level, and it looks across at the fine peak of Ekbhai, which is more than 1,000 feet higher. In the south of Dera Ghazi Khan district the general level of the chain is low and the Giandari hill, only 4,160 feet above the sea level, stand, out conspicuously. Finally, where the three jurisdictions met the hills melt into the Kachh Gandava plain. Kaisargarh is a fine limestone mountain crowned by a forest of the edible chilgoza pine. But the ordinary tree growth, where found at all, is of a much humbler kind, consisting of gnarled olives and dwarf palms.

Passes and Torrents in Sulaiman Hills

The drainage of the western slopes of the Sulaiman range finding no exit on that side has had to wear out ways for itself towards the plains which lay between the foot of the hills and the Indus. This was the explanation of the large number of passage, about one hundred, which lead from the plains into the Sulaiman hills. The chief from north to south were the Vehoa, the Sangarh, the Khair, the Kaha, the Chachar, and the Siri, called from the torrents which flowed through them to the plains. There was an easy route through the Chachar to Balochistan. But unfortunately the water of the torrent was blackish.

Sub-Himalaya or Shivaliks

In its lowest ridges the Himalaya drop to a height of about 5,000 feet. But the traveller to any of the summer resorts in the mountains passes through a zone of lower hills interspersed sometimes with valleys or 'duns'. These consist of tertiary sandstones, clays, and boulder conglomerates, the debris in fact which the Himalaya has dropped in the course of ages. To this group of hills and valleys the general name of Shivaliks is given. East of the Jhelum it includes the Nahan hills to the north of Ambala the low hills of Kangra, Hoshiarpur, Gurdaspur, and Jammu, and the Pabbi hills in Gujarat. But it is to the west of the Jhelum that the system has its

1. The Deputy Commissioner of Dera Ghazi Khan and the Commissioner of Multan used to spend part of the hot-weather at Fort Munro.

greatest extension. Practically the whole of the soil of the plains of Attock, Rawalpindi, and Jhelum districts consists of disintegrated Shivalik sandstone, and differs widely in appearance and agricultural quality from the alluvium of the true Panjab plains. The low hills of the districts belong to the same system, but the Salt Range is only in part Shivalik. Altogether Shivalik deposits in the Panjab cover an area of 13,000 square miles. Beyond the Indus the hills of the Kohat district and a part of the Sulaiman range are of tertiary age.

The Great Panjab Plain

The passage from the highlands to the plains is as a rule abrupt, and the contrast between the two is extraordinary. This is true without qualification of the tract between the Jamna and the Jhelum. It is equally true of British districts west of the Jhelum and south of the Salt Range and of lines drawn from Kalabagh on the west bank of the Indus southwards to Paniala and thence north-west through the Pezu pass to the Waziristan hills. In this vast plain, if we accept the insignificant hills in extreme south-west of the province ending to the north in the historic ridge at Delhi, some hillocks of gneiss near Tosham in Hissar, and the curious little isolated rocks at Kirana, Chiniot, and Sangal near the Chenab and Jhelum, the only eminences are petty ridges of windblown sand and the "*Thehs*" or mounds which represent the accumulated debris of ancient village sites. At the end of the Jurassic period and later this great plain was part of a sea bed. Far removed as the Indian ocean now is the height above sea level of the Panjab plain east of the Jhelum is nowhere above 1,000 feet. Delhi and Lahore are both just above the 700 feet line. The hills mentioned above are humble time-worn outliers of the very ancient Aravalli system, to which the hills of Rajasthan belong. Kirana and Sangla were already of enormous age, when they were islands washed by the waves of the Tertiary sea.

The Salt Range

The tract west of the Jhelum, and bounded on the south by the Salt Range cis-Indus, and trans-Indus by the lines already mentioned, is of a more varied character. Time worn though the Salt Range has become by the waste of ages, it still rises at Sakesar[1], near its western

1. Sakesar or Sukesar is a Hill sanatorium, 5,010 feet, on the highest peak of Salt Range, in Shahpur district.

extremity, to a height of 5,000 feet. The eastern part of the range is mostly in the Jhelum district, and there the highest point is Chail.[1] The hill of Tilla[2], which is a marked feature of the landscape looking westwards from Jhelum cantonment, is on a spur running north-east from the main chain. The Salt Range is poorly wooded, the dwarf acacia[3] or Acacia modesta[4], the olive, and the sanattan shrub[5] are the commonest species. But these jagged and arid hills include some not infertile valleys, every inch of which is put under crop by the crowded population. To geologists the range is of special interest, including as it does at one end of the scale Cambrian beds of enormous antiquity and at the other rocks of Tertiary age. Embedded in the Cambrianstrata there are great deposits of rock salt at Kheora[6], where the Mayo mine is situated. At Kalabagh the Salt Range reappears on the far side of the Indus. Here the salt comes to the surface, and its jagged pinnacles present a remarkable appearance.

Country North of the Salt Range

The country to the north of the Salt Range included in the districts of Jhelum, Rawalpindi, and Attock is often ravine-bitten and seamed with the white sandy beds of torrents. Generally speaking, it is an arid precarious tract but there are fertile stretches. The general height of the plains north of the Salt Range is from 1,000 feet to 2,000 feet above sea level. The rise between Lahore and Rawalpindi is just over a thousand feet. Low Hills usually form a feature of the landscape, pleasing at a distance or when softened by the evening light, but bare and jagged on a nearer view. The chief hills are the Margalla range between Hazara and Rawalpindi, the Kalachitta and the Khairimurat hills running east and west through

1. 3,700 feet.
2. 3,242 feet. A notable place in the Salt Range is known as Jogi Tillah. The elevation, and consequent coolness of the climate, have made it a kind of summer resort and Sanatorium for the civil officers of Jhelum and the neighbourhood.
3. Kikkar.
4. Phulahi.
5. Do donea Viscoss.
6 Kheowra in Jhelum District, in Salt Range. There is a fort and temple on a spur of the Salt Range (*Archaeological Survey Report* Vol. V. pp. 85-90).

Attock and the very dry and broken Narrara hills on the right bank of the Indus in the same district. Between the Margalla and Kala-chitta hills is the Margalla pass on the main road from Rawalpindi to the passage of the Indus at Attock, and, therefore, a position of considerable strategical importance. The Kalachitta[1] chain is so called because the north side is formed of nummullitic limestone and the south mainly of a dark purple sandstone. The best tree-growth is therefore on the north side. Across the Indus the Peshawar and Bannu districts are basins ringed hills and drained respectively by the Kabul and Kurram rivers with their affluents. Between these two basins lies the maze of bare broken hills and valleys which make up the Kohat district.

Rivers and Their Importance

All the seven great rivers of the Panjab, viz., the Indus, the Jhelum. the Chenab, the Ravi, the Beas, the Satluj and the Ghaggar, rise in the Himalayas, and after long courses, sometimes of several hundred miles, amid snow-clad ranges, they debouch on the plains. The slope of the low country is to the south and south-west, and is very gradual, seldom exceeding two feet in a mile ; and this determines the course of the rivers. In the process of time each stream has cut for itself a wide valley, which lies well below the level of the plain, and whose banks mark the extreme limits of the course on either side. Within this valley the river meanders in a narrow but ill-defined and ever-shifting channel. In the winter the stream is comparatively small ; but as the mountain snows melt at the approach of the hot season, the waters rise and overflow the surrounding country, often to a distance of several miles on either side. At the close of the rainy season, the waters recede, leaving wide expanses of fertile loam for less fertile sand.

Of these seven rivers the Indus is the largest. Already a mighty stream when it emerges from the Hazara hills, it flows almost due south past Attock. Here it pierces the Salt Range. Thus far it forms the western boundary ; but south of Kalabagh it enters Province, and divides the Isa Khel tahsil of Mianwali from the rest of that District. Farther south again it forms the western boundary until it re-enters

1. Black and white.

Panjab territory near Bhakkar, and divides Dera Ghazi Khan from Mianwali and Muzaffargarh districts and from the State of Bahawalpur.

The Jhelum enters the Panjab east of the Salt Range, flowing south between to it and the Pabbi hills, which terminate at Mong Rasul. Thence the river flows west, and then south until it is joined by the Chenab near Jhang.

The Chenab rises in the Himalayan canton of Lahul within the Province, and after traversing the erstwhile Chamba State and the Jammu province of Kashmir debouches on the plains east of the Jhelum, into which it falls about two hundred and twenty-five miles from the hills.

The Ravi, rising in Chamba, reaches the plain below Dalhousie, and joins the combined waters of the Jhelum and Chenab fifty miles south of Jhang. The united streams of these three rivers form the Trimab.

The Beas, rising on the south of the Rohtang pass on the opposite side of the Central Himalaya to the Ravi, traverses the Kulu valley southward, and then bends suddenly westward, through the Mandi State and Kangra District, until it turns the northern flank of the Shivaliks, and enters the plains within a few miles of the Ravi. Thence its course is more southerly, and it falls into the Satluj about seventy miles from its debouchure.

The Satluj rising near the source of Indus in Tibet, enters the Province near the Shipki pass, traverses Bashahr and other States of the Simla Hills, and pierces the Shivaliks near Ropar. Thence it runs almost due west to its junction with the Beas near Sobraon where it takes a more southerly course for two hundred and seventy miles, and falls into the Trimab, nine miles north of Uch. Below this confluence the waters of the Jhelum, Chenab, and Ravi, Satluj and Beas form the Panjnad or 'five rivers' ; which falls into the Indus at Mithankot.

The Ghaggar rises in the territory of Nahan and, passing through Morni, leaves the hills by the Chandgarh gorge. Thence it passes on into Patiala territory, but again touches the border of the district at a short distance to the west of the city of Ambala. Near Mani Majra it is largely used to irrigate the Kharar Neli circle. The water being drawn off by means of artificial cuts or 'kuls'. The bed is covered with large boulders for a few miles below the hills, but soon becomes a wide tract of sand. The upper portion of the course contains water throughout the year a foot deep in summer, but reaching six feet or more in the rains, and when in flood, the current is very dangerous to cross. The Sarusti, the ancient Saraswati, is famous in the annals of early Brahminical history as the most sacred river in India after the Ganges. It does not rise in the hills, but begins in a large depression at Kalawar in the north of the Mustafabad pargana of Jagadhri. The phenomenon, however, seems amply explained by the supposition that anciently the Ghaggar was considered an affluent of the Sarusti, instead of the Sarusti of Ghaggar ; and that when ancient writers speak of the Sarusti, they included under that name the united Ghaggar and Sarusti.

These seven rivers which make the plain of the Panjab so rich and fertile has often been compared with the fertile plain of Egypt, which has equally been benefited by the Nile river. It is stated that "If Egypt is a gift of Nile, the plain of the Panjab is a gift of the Himalayas". We have seen above that all these seven rivers are the gift of the Himalayas.

2

The Board of Administration (1849-1853)

Annexation of the Panjab

When Lord Hardinge,[1] in the hope of preserving the Sikh Kingdom concluded the Treaty of Lahore, he was far from confident of the ultimate success of his scheme ; but "considering the importance of the results aimed at" he believed it to be worth trying. "I confess," he wrote to Henry Lawrence, "I think the probability is against the continuance of a Sikh Government ;" and on March 11, 1846, he thus concluded his address to the assembled Sardars : "Success or failure is in your own hands ; my co-operation shall not be wanting ; but if you neglect this opportunity, no aid on the part of the British Government can save the State."

Reasons

Lord Hardinge did not annex the Panjab for two reasons ; in the first place respect was paid to the memory of Maharaja Ranjit Singh, the old and faithful ally of Great Britain ; and secondly he doubted whether he was strong enough to occupy the whole country. Shorn of their territory, and limited as to the size of the regular army they might maintain, the Sikhs were given one more chance to preserve their national existence[2]. But the British Government by the treaties of March 8 and 11, 1846, had already taken possession of

---

1. Lord Hardinge (1844-1848) was a brave soldier and was well acquainted with the arts of war and peace. He was the hero of the Peninsular war and had participated in battle of Waterloo.
2. A History of British India—P.E. Roberts, p. 338.

the richest districts of the Panjab to the south and north of the Satluj. They had transferred the hill territories to their friend Raja Gulab Singh and carried away a large number of Sikh guns. They had disbanded a large portion of the Sikh army and so reduced its strength as to render it absolutely helpless even for the purposes of internal peace and order. The Panjab troops had been removed from within the city of Lahore and the British force placed in full possession of the fort and the city, with the Maharaja and the Queen-mother at their mercy.

Political Aspect

The British had stirred up the forntier Muslim tribes against the Sikhs and their government. They could only retain their sympathies and attachment by the subversion of the Sikh Kingdom and occupying the country themselves to be able to reward them. For a whole century the Muslims of the Western Panjab served as henchmen of the British against all progressive movements in the country and were, in the end, richly rewarded by their patrons with the grant of Pakistan in 1947.

And, above all, with the Sikhs removed from the Panjab, the British, sitting at the mouth of the Afghan passes, could with greater ease and facility watch the politics of Afghanistan, move up their armies when necessary, and strengthen their defences against the dreaded Cossacks of Russia. Lord Dalhousie's action was not approved unanimously by those in authority then. One of his own Councellors, Sir George Clark, expressed strong disagreement with his policy of annexation. The Directors did not approve of Dalhousie's action ungrudgingly and unanimously. The despatch registering the approval of the annexation was signed by thirteen members while the seven members recorded their dissent.

Lord Dalhousie an Annexationist

Sardars Chattar Singh and Sher Singh surrendered at Hurmuk to General Gilbert on March 10, 1849, and four days later, on the 14th, at Rawalpindi the Sikh soldiers with tears in their eyes, kissed their swords and laid them down never to see them again, exclaiming, with choked throats : Today Ranjit Singh is dead. Sir Henry Lawrence was deadly against the annexation of the Panjab. Lord Dalhousie therefore selected his foreign Secretary Henry M. Elliot as his agent for the final transaction. Under the instructions from the Governor-General of India, Mr. Elliot saw the members of the Council of Regency privately, in the first instance, and made it clear to them on March 28, 1849, "that any reluctance on the part would be a great mistake, that the Maharaja as well as themselves would be sufferers from it, that Governor-General in any case be carried out the only difference being that if they, with the Maharaja gave their formal assent, the advantageous position they then held would be guaranteed to them, while if they would lose everything which the British government chose to resume.

The Proclamation

On March 29, 1849 A.D., Sir Henry Elliot, the Foreign Secretary, held a Darbar[1] at Lahore for the purpose of making known the decision of the Government of India. It was attended by the boy-Maharaja[2] seated, for the last time, on the throne of his ancestors. All the Sikh chiefs were present in the capital, while the proceedings were watched by a vast concourse of spectators. The proclamation was a most artful piece of speciosity full of misleading and wrong statements. It said :

"The British have faithfully kept their word and have scrupulously observed every obligation which the treaties imposed upon them.

"But the Sikh people and their chiefs have, on their part, grossly and faithlessly violated the premises by which they were bound.

"Of their annual tribute no portion whatever has at any time been paid and large loans advanced to them by the Government of India have never been repaid...

"Finally, the army of the state, and the whole Sikh people, joined by many of the Sardars in the Panjab, who signed the treaties, and led by a member of the Regency itself have risen in arms against us and have waged a force and bloody war, for the proclaimed purpose

1. The Lawrence of Lucknow—Morreson, p. 224.
2. Maharaja Dalip Singh, the only surviving son of Maharaja Ranjit Singh.

of destroying the British and their power."[1]

Amidst a deep silence, the Proclamation of the Annexation of the Panjab was read aloud in English, Persian and Hindustani. In the equally deep silence which followed, a paper was then handed by Tej Singh[2] (the traitor) to the Maharaja, containing the conditions on which he and his chiefs might assure themselves of generous treatment at the hands of their conquerors. The paper was immediately signed by Dalip Singh, of course under compulsion, after which Sir Henry Elliot rose and left the hall. As he did so the British flag was hoisted on the ramparts of the Lahore citadel, and the booming of guns announced that the Kingdom of Lahore had ceased to exist.

It is impossible to study the history of the Sikhs during the last decade of their kingdom's existence without being led to share Lord Dalhousie's conviction of the "expediency, the justice, and the necessity" of the annexation. The considerations which determined his policy can be best summarized by quoting from the Proclamation itself.

"The Government of India formerly declared that it desired no further conquests, and it proved by its act the sincerity of its professions." The Government of India has no desire for conquests now : but it is bound in its duty to provide fully for its own security, and to guard the interests of those committed to its charge." "To that end, and as the only mode of protecting the State from the perpetual recurrence of unprovoked and wasting wars, the Governor-General is compelled to resolve upon the entire subjection of a people whom their own government had long been unable to control, and whom no punishment could deter from violence and no acts of friendship could conciliate to peace." "Therefore the Governor-General had declared and hereby proclaims, that the Kingdom of the Panjab is at the end ; and that all the territories of Maharaja Dalip Singh are now and henceforth a portion of the British Empire in India."

---

1. Dalhousie's Administration, Arnold, pp. 202-204. History of the Panjab, Latif, pp. 572-573.
2. Tej Singh's original name was Tej Ram. He was Brahman from Meerut District and was a nephew of Jamadar Khushal Singh. He took service in the Lahore Court in 1811, when he was of 12 years of age. To please Maharaja Ranjit Singh he embraced Sikhism, in 1816 A.D. and became Tej Singh.

The instrument by which the Panjab was declared annexed, was a 'treaty' concluded by the Maharaja's government, and the Honourable East India Company, and ratified by the Governor-General of India on April 5, 1849 A.D. It consisted of five Articles. By its terms :

1st.—His Highness the Maharaja Dalip Singh shall resign for himself, his heirs, and his successors, all rights title, and claim to the sovereignty of the Panjab, or to any sovereign power whatever.

2nd.—All the property of the State, of whatever description and wheresover found, shall be confiscated to the Honourable East India Company, in part payment of the debt due by the State of Lahore to the British Government, and of the expenses of the war.

3rd.—The Gem called the Koh-i-noor, which was taken from Shah Shujah-ul-Mulk by Maharaja Ranjit Singh, shall be surrendered by the Maharaja of Lahore to the Queen of England.

4th.—His Highness Dalip Singh shall receive from the Honourable East India Company, for the support of himself, his relatives and the servants of the State, a pension not less than four and not exceeding five lakhs of company's rupees per annum.

5th.—His Highness shall be treated with respect and honour. He shall retain the title of Maharaja Dalip Singh Bahadur, and he shall continue to receive, during his life, such portion of the above named pension as may be allotted to himself personally, provided he shall remain obedient to British Government, and shall reside at such place as the Governor-General of India may select.[1]

Thus the Panjab "which had been for centuries the tempting lure of a succession of invading hordes and a prey to anarchy passed like its framed "Mountain of Light" into the possessions of Queen Victoria. · The British government was eager to annex the Panjab, also on account of its economic as well as political aspects. The cotton of the Panjab was one of the chief attractions to the British who foresaw in the land of five rivers a favourable market for the

1. Granted and accepted at Lahore, on the 29th of March 1849, and ratified by the Honourable the Governor-General on the 5th April 1849. (Sd). 1. Dalhousie, L.S 2. H.H. Elliot L.S. 3. H.M. Lawrence, L.S. 4. Maharaja Dalip Singh. 5. Raja Tej Singh. 6. Dina Nath. 6. Bhai Nidhan Singh. 7. Nur-ud-din. 8. Gundur Singh, Agent of Sher Singh Sindhanwalla. 9. Sardar Lall Singh, Agent and son of Sardar Attar Singh Kalianwala.

consumption of their goods. While Amritsar offered the prospects of an enterpot for the Panjab and the hill territories of Jammu and Kashmir, Multan and Peshawar promised to become advanced depots for British trade in Afghanistan and in regions beyond the Oxus.

The Panjab also offered vast opportunities of employment for a large number of British civilians and politicals with handsome salaries, allowances, furloughs and pensions. It also offered facilities of extensive cantonments and mountainous training—grounds for the British troops.

Justification of the Annexation

There was no rising either of the army or the people in the central Sikh districts of the state ; not a single British officer was attacked or molested. The British Resident continued to stay at the capital of the kingdom issuing orders to the Council of Regency. The Darbar, was providing the fullest co-operation. Only one member of the Regency, out of eight had joined the rebels and another was only suspected. The remaining six were perfectly faithful and obedient. In addition to the great majority of the army who took no part in the revolt, "at least 20,000 subjects of Lahore State," according to Major Bell, "enrolled in its service, fought on the side of the British Government, and assisted in suppressing the rebellion," not knowing that at the end their country would be annexed and permanently occupied by the British Government.

The Darbar had trusted the good faith of the British Government and relied upon the treaty of December 16, 1846, which was to 'have effect during the minority of His Highness Maharaja Dalip Singh, and cease and terminate on His Highness attaining the full age of sixteen years, or on the 4th September, 1854'. But five years and a half before the due date, when their ward, the Maharaja, was yet a minor, being only eleven years of age, Lord Dalhousie broke his faith and cheated him out of his kingdom.

There is little more to be told. Maharaja Dalip Singh was granted permission to reside wherever he chose in British territory outside the Panjab. His final act of submission was to surrender the

Koh-i-nur[1] to the British Government. The precious gem, after lying forgotten for some weeks in the waistcoat pocket of Johan Lawrence, was sent to England, where its adventures had terminated. It was presented to Queen Victoria, together with a letter from Lord Dalhousie containing a complete record of the vicissitudes through which the Koh-i-nur had passed.

Rani Jindan

Rani Jindan, the youngest wife of Maharaja Ranjit Singh and the mother of Maharaja Dalip Singh was variously known as Maharani, Rani, Mai and the queen mother, but she was popularly called Rani Jindan. She was the daughter of one Manna Singh, an Aulakh Jat, who hailed from village Chhachar Gujranwala District. Her father, Manna Singh served as a junior officer (Kumedan) on the establishment of Ranjit Singh. She was born in 1817 and was very beautiful as well as charming.

Jindan was, no doubt, a clever and ambitious woman, but her power to influence Darbar politics since Bhairowal, had been highly exaggerated. In November, 1846, Hardinge had issued instructions that she must be deprived of all political powers[2]. She had played a prominent role in the plot in which Raja Hira Singh had been assassinated. She had also instigated the Sikh soldierty to cross the Satluj in 1845 in the First Anglo-Sikh war. Though Bhairowal had clipped her wings, she was still considered powerful by the government for mischief. "If a good opportunity must occur," Hardinge wrote in March 1847[3], "she must be sent away from Lahore, but up to this moment, the insurrection of her ill temper had not been so greatly felt as to justify a harsh remedy without a good cause".[4]

1. This world famous diamond, taken originally from the mines of Kollur, was, in 1656 A.D. presented by Mir Jumla at that time the Wazir of Golconda, to the Emperor, Shah Jahan. In 1739 A.D., it formed part of plunder which Nadir Shah carried away with him to Iran. On the murder of the Shah at Kelat, in 1747 A.D. it passed to his grandson, Shah Rukh, by whom, four years later, it was presented to Ahmed Shah Abdali, the founder of the Durrani dynasty at Kabul. It came into possession of Shah Zaman, in 1793 and of Shah Shuja in 1795 A.D.
2. Lahore Political Diaries, Vol. III, 9 February, 1847 ; and 10 June, 1847.
3. Governor-General to Currie (Foreign Secretary) 23 Nov. 1846 A.D.
4. Hardinge to Hobhouse, 21 March, 1847.

A few months later, it was considered necessary to keep her baneful influence away from the young Maharaja. "It is a measure", Hardinge said, "for the welfare of the boy under British guardianship."[1]

Rani Jindan Suspected

Soon an opportunity occurred. At an investiture Darbar held in August, 1847, the young Maharaja refused to pronounce Tej Singh as the Raja of Sialkot. There was neither any justification nor occasion for it, but the Resident had browbeaten the Council in accepting the proposal, which had originated from the Government of India. Embarrassment was caused, but Lawrence performed the investiture ceremony himself. Immediately afterwards, he accused that Rani Jindan had instigated the young Maharaja to insult Tej Singh[2]. It was also alleged that she was training up her son as an instrument of hatred against the Darbar, and instilling in his mind sentiments of aversion against the Resident and the Council. "Maharaja Dalip Singh", Hardinge commented, "be removed from the debasing influence of such a mother."[3]

Under Strict British Surveillance

At the same time the Queen mother was suspected of having a hand in what is known as the 'Preyma Plot'. In February, Preyma, an ex-commandant of Gulab Singh's service and a soldier of fortune, came to Lahore and started intriguing with various officers and sepoys of the Sikh Corps. A conspiracy came to light, in which it was alleged that Preyma and his accomplices designed to murder the British Resident and the Sikh Commander-in-Chief, Tej Singh, on the occasion of fete at the Shalamar Gardens. John Lawrence, who conducted an enquiry found the evidence in the case 'worthless', without any evidence of the Rani's complicity. But he held that there were grounds for suspecting her of being cognizant of the intrigue if not its instigator.

On these grounds, it was considered desirable to remove her from the capital. The Darbar, however, hesitated to share the odium of her expulsion from the Panjab, but it agreed to her removal to

1. Hardinge to Hobhouse, 14 August, 1847.
2. Resident to Government, 7 August, 1847, XLI, 1849 A. D.
3. Governor-General to Secret Committee, 5 Sept., 1847.

Shaikhupura[1]. At the same time, her allowance under the Agreement of December, 1846, was reduced to Rs. 48,000.

Jindan Deported

Since Jindan's removal to Shaikhupura in September, 1847, Rani Jindan had been living under strict British surveillance, but she was still considered a woman of great resolution who could sway the Sikh armies. Because of the fear that she might raise a general revolt in the Panjab, Dalhousie had instructed Currie to expel her unceremoniously from the Panjab. Currie acted, before Dalhousie's instructions reached him. He implicated her in the plot, and her allowance reduced to Rs. 4,000 a month, and contrary to the advice of the Council removed her to Ferozepur "before a soul knew about her removal." She was sent to Benaras with the warning, that if she was detected intriguing in state matters any more, she would be shut up in the fortress of Chunar. Newspapers commented that she had been whisked away from Shaikhupura by a stratagem.[2] Dalhousie's approbation of Currie's action is significant : "Nothing could have been better planned, more speedily and more secretly or better executed than the removal of the Maharani with the sanction of the Darbar. You have got rid of a serious danger by that act."[3]

Jindan's political influence on the Panjab affairs was unduly magnified even long after her deportation to Benaras, when her allowance was further reduced to Rs. 1,000 per month and restrictions involving ill treatment and indignity were placed upon her. "Her memory survived, for she was not a woman to be forgotton;" observed Herbert Edwardes, "but her influence had followed her power and there was no longer a man bound in the Panjab who would shoulder a musket at her bidding."[4] But Dalhousie considered her a great menace : "rely upon it, she is worth more than all the soldiers of the state put together, for any purpose of mischief."[5] The news of her banishment gave the Jat soldiery ample grounds for resentment. To the Sikh population, as a whole, it appeared as a national affront.

1. 25 miles away from Lahore.
2. Dalhousie to Hobhouse, 2 June, 1848.
3. Dolhousie to Currie (Private), 28 May, 1848.
4. A Year on the Panjab Frontier, Vol. II, p. 142.
5. Dalhousie to Hobhouse, 3 January, 1848.

While her presence in the Panjab would have passed unnoticed, her exile provided a cause of disaffection among the troops at Multan and Hazara.

The Rani Escaped From Chunar

It was reported that Rani Jindan had escaped from the fortress of Chunar. Since her deportation from Panjab in May, 1848 A.D., she had been interned at Benaras under strict guard; and though a woman of great resolution and ability, she had been content to live on a reduced allowance and restrictions involving ill treatment and indignity. During the Panjab campaign, however, allegations were made by Major Macregor, in attendance on her, that she was in correspondence both with Dewan Mulraj and Raja Sher Singh. A few of her letters were intercepted and an alarm was created when some of her slave girls escaped from Benaras. On these grounds it was decided to remove her to the fortress of Chunar. The manner of her escape could not be ascertained, and it was even doubtful whether she had at all arrived there.

The news was well received at Calcutta. Dalhousie reported home, that her escape had merely caused an annoyance, and the matter was of no importance.[1]

Jindan reached Kathmandu on April 29, 1849. The Nepalese Court held her arrival rather unexpected and undesired, but Jang Bahadur, the Prime-Minister, after some hesitation, granted her asylum mainly in consideration of respect for the memory of late Maharaja Ranjit Singh.[2]

Not Well-Treated in Nepal

The British Resident at Kathmandu reported the matter to Calcutta. A demand for her surrender was considered inexpedient because of a fear of quarrel with Nepal; the Government of India

1. "I have confiscated her 9 lacs worth of jewels, and she had no money of her own, so that she can't do much harm. If she flies to Nepal and keeps quiet there, it will be a clear gain, for she would lose her pension of course. If she goes to Panjab she can do no mischief now. Three months ago it would have been less agreeable."
(Dalhousie to Hobhouse, 2 May, 1849.)
2. Nicholette's Narrative of Principal Events in Nepal (1849)—Nepal Residency Papers.

contented itself by addressing a communication to the Court of Nepal to take effective measures to prevent her engaging in political intrigues[1]. The Home Government also expressed delight at her escape. "The flight of the Rani," Dalhousie was informed, "is just, what you call it, "rather annoying than important." In some respects it is rather useful than otherwise. You will get and save money by it, and be spared of the custody of a cunning, good-for-nothing woman."[2]

British records relate the details of her rather unhappy sojourn in Nepal till 1860 A.D. Although, for political reasons no demand for her surrender could be made, yet the British Resident at Kathmandu was directed to keep a vigilant eye upon her. Jindan settled in comfort, though not in a small house at Thapathali, near Jang Bahadur's residence. She devoted herself to a life of religious devotion and charity, but it soon became evident, that the British Residency would not leave her in peace. A whispering campaign soon started against her imaginary conspiracies, and bubbles of political intrigues against the British were blown up. It was alleged that she was a dangerous woman, engaged in organising political disaffection against the British and the revival of the Sikh dynasty in the Panjab. All this of course baseless, but the steady pressure of the British functionaries in Nepal, led to the gradual antagonisation of the Nepalese Darbar against her, culminating in the imposition of most humiliating restrictions on her.

But neither the misdirected zeal of the British officials at Kathmandu, nor the hostility, and indifference of the Nepalese Court, could break her spirit. After a decade of exile and isolation, she still retained her bold and imperious disposition. She patiently protested against the indignities and restrictions placed upon her by Jang Bahadur until 1860 A.D., when she could brook them no longer. As the Nepal Residency records tell us an open rift occurred between her and Jang Bahadur, and "several scenes occurred in which each seems to have given way to temper to have addressed the other in very insulting language.

---

1. Dalhousie to Hobhouse, 11 May, 1849.
2. Indian Board letter, 23 June, 1849.

Towards the end of 1860 A.D. it was signified to Rani Jindan that her son Maharaja Dalip singh was about to return to India and that she could visit him in Calcutta. She was already tired of living in isolation in Nepal, and being fed up with the indignities imposed upon her by Jang Bahadur, she readily welcomed the opportunity of joining her son, whom she accompanied in 1861 to England. There, two years later, she died.

A Review on Rani Jindan

A critical review on Rani Jindan is necessary here to assess her responsibility to lose the Sikh kingdom or to see whether she was actually *"More sinned against than sinning"*. Jindan's passions over-mastered her reason, coloured her vision, and led her to embark on course of action that was wanton, wayward, bereft of all political sagacity and statesmanship. Headstrong, though not whimsical, the Queen-mother lacked patience, tact, caution and an ability to manoeuver political events and situations to her advantage. It was not in her character to win over men and parties and use them to strengthen her position. In the delicate situation prevailing in the Panjab in those days, she behaved more like an autocrat ruler than like a shrewd and far-seeing statesman. It cannot be emphasised at the same time that had she been endowed with all the requisite qualities of a wise ruler, she would have controlled and mastered the situation around her. Her army generals, too, were intolerant and exhibited a complete lack of political understanding of the situation then prevailing *vis-a-vis* the advancing frontiers of the British empire. There were thus three factors which contended against each other in that epoch making period of the Indian History :

1. The character and the temperament of Maharani of the Panjab.

2. The mutual hostilities among the generals born out of their political ambitions.

3. The fast advancing frontiers of the British empire and anxiety of the British to extend their empire upto Balochistan and N.W.F.P. because of the fear of France and Russia who might, it was feared, make invasions into the Indian territory from the North. The British statesmanship after their bitter lesson against Dost Muhammad,

regarded the entire border in the North as vulnerable and a breeding ground for all types of hostile forces.

Considering the third point first, regarding the attitude of the British towards the Lahore Darbar, we, as faithful students of history, must take into account :

1. The political ethics of those times.

2. Whether the Britishers acted solely in self interest when they finally thought of annexing the Panjab.

3. Or, whether they watched the situation coolly and stepped in only on the open invitation of the Queen, or by arriving at a secret understanding with some of the Generals of the Sikh army.

4. Again, whether they found the situation so fluid, and not boiling that they could not but intervene, that any other power, however, sympathetic and sincere towards the Lahore Darbar, would have also acted in the manner the British did.

The first two points in fact attracted the third one as enumerated above. Looking upon the three factors objecting it appears that it was the character of Jindan that moulded the course of history, and not so much the other two factors. It was the Queen's personality which brought about a succession of events which weakened and disintegrated the Sikh empire beyond redemption. It is Rani Jindan who can be held solely responsible for the downfall of the Khalsa. In spite of everything, hers was a unique personality. She was neither a draft, nor dolt, but she exerted her influence and used her political power so fast and quick that she could not even count the events, her actions gave birth, to let aside her assessing the situation as a whole and fore-seeing the consequences of what we may call now her misdeeds.

Everything in her hand misfired and boomranged upon her. In her desperation, she took recourse to the British help who were only eagerly waiting round the corner to grab such a golden opportunity. Since the Queen, despite her faults and follies, saddled the political horse so tightly under her legs that the horse itself perished underneath her fast hold. It was not in her character to play up the political cards with tact, caution and wisdom. The result was that the

British as soon as they got into the arena on this side of the Satluj (river) they at once began to tighten the strings around the Queen's neck.

THE BOARD OF ADMINISTRATION 1849-1853

The battle of Gujarat placed the coping stone on the edifice of British empire in India. The last Indian principality valiantly fought a lone battle to preserve its independence but fortune once more favoured the ever victorious English. "The power and spirit of Ranjit Singh's great armament, terrific in the death throes of its expiring wrath"[1] were utterly crushed. On the 12th March, 1849, Sardar Chattar Singh, Raja Sher Singh and thirtyfive chiefs surrendered before General Gilbert and laid down their arms.

The Triumvirate

After the British annexation decided on by Lord Dalhousie the administration of the Panjab was placed in the hands of Board, consisting of Sir Henry Lawrence as President, Mr. John Lawrence[2] and Mr. Mansel both of the Civil Service as members, generally known as 'the triumvirate'. Under them were placed several young British civil and military officers, chosen for the services by Lord Dalhousie. Henry Lawrence was already well acquainted with the Panjab and her Sardars and soldiers, having commanded a contingent of Sikh troops that had accompanied General Pollock's force to Kabul in 1842 A.D.

1. Henry Lawrence, President

At the head of the Administration Board came the man Sir Henry Lawrence who had filled the highest post in the Panjab before its annexation first as Resident. That he was appointed to the first place in the administration of the new province, is almost as creditable to a man of the autocratic tendencies of Lord Dalhousie as to Henry Lawrence himself. He had already had many a short brush with Lord Dalhousie and there was an antagonism between the two men which each had felt that no amount of mutual forbearance could bridge over. However, Lord Dalhousie was wise enough to respect

1. History of India, Vol. III-Marshman, p. 346.
2. Afterwards Lord Lawrence of the Panjab.

and to trust those from whom he differed, if he knew that they had the root of the matter in them.

Had Lord Dalhousie been anxious to clear Henry Lawrence out of his path and to put somebody else in his place who would prove a mere-tool in his hands, it would have been easy for him to do so. For Henry Lawrence, finding that his scruples against annexation had been finally overruled, voluntarily placed his resignation in Lord Dalhousie's hands, and would certainly have carried his purpose out had not Lord Dalhousie urged him to reconsider it, on the unanswerable plea that the objects dearest to his heart could not be thwarted and might be furthered by him remaining at Lahore.

Distribution of work among the Triumvirate

Henry Lawrence, on whose shoulders fell the task of enforcing the new policy was, by far, the best man that could have been selected for this purpose. He had come into close contact with Sikh politics since 1840, as a political assistant, first at Ludhiana, and then at Ferozepur. He understood the Sikhs well, as also their virtues and vices. Since March 1846, he had seen to the fulfilment of the treaty. Lawrence wielded enormous powers, but he resisted Hardinge's insistence on active interference everywhere.[1]

A sense of moderation guided him in his dealings with the Sikhs, whose national traits he understood so well. He eschewed overbearance, desisted from overriding the Darbar's nominal authority, but enforced his decisions judiciously, by the employment of Sikh agency under British political officers in practically all the districts. His newly formed Council[2] had a system of portfolios. The army was split up into regular and irregular forces, a Public Works Department was created, and a Sikh ecclasiastical portfolio was placed under Bhai Nidhan Singh.

2. John Lawrence, member

Next-to Sir Henry Lawrence on the Board, came Henry

1. Resident to Secretary to Governor-General, 21 June, 1887—(pp) XLI. 1849.
2. 6 Sikhs, 1 Hindu, 1 Muslim members.

Lawrence's brother John[1]. His knowledge of Sikh races was only less than that of his brother ; while in mastery of details, financial skill, in power of continuous work, and in general civil training, he was far superior to him. A man who had ruled the Jullundur Doab during the last two years in the way in which John Lawrence had ruled it, and with the results which the prolonged and doubtful struggle of the Second Sikh war was brought into full relief, was clearly this man to have a potential voice in the rule of the four other Doabs which the fortune of war and then thrown over.

3. Mansel, member

But a Board must consist of more than two members, and Charles Grevile Mansel,[2] the third member, was a man equable and philosophic temperament than either of the Lawrences. Like John, he was a civilian who had served his apprenticeship in the North-West. He was a man of contemplation rather than of action, and it was perhaps well that he was so ; for the two brothers with all their high mental gifts...were pre-eminently men of action. Mensel thus served as foil to them both, in a different sense from that in which they served as a foil to each other.

Mansel was admirably fitted to discover the weak points in any course of action which was proposed, and, with somewhat irritating impartiality, would argue with John in favour of Henry's views, and with Henry in favour of John's. He would thus throw the "dry light of the intellect" on questions which might otherwise had been seen, owing either to the aristocratic leanings of

1. Lawrence—John Laird Mair, first Baron Lawrence (1811-1879), Governor-General of India, sixth son and eight of twelve children of Lieutenant-Colonel Alexander Lawrence, and younger brother of Sir Henry Montgomery Lawrence and Sir Geroge St. Patrick Lawrence, was born at Richmond in Yorkshire, where his father's regiment (the 19th foot) was then quartered, on 4 March, 1811.
2. Mansel, Charles Grenville (1806-1886), Indian official, born in 1806, was appointed a writer in the East India Company's service on 20th April, 1826. He was acting magistrate of Agra in 1830; joint magistrate and deputy collector of Agra, 15 Nov., 1831, From 1844 to 1849 he was on furlough, and on his return to India was appointed member of the Board of Administration for the affairs of the Panjab, under the Presidency of Sir Henry Lawrence. He died at 7 Mills Terrace, West Brighton, on 19 Nov, 1886.

Henry or the democratic leanings of John, through a too highly coloured medium. If he was not good at carrying out into action any views of his colleagues, which they might have been anxious in the exuberance of their energy, to carry out at once, often passed, owing to his idiosyncrasies, through a sifting process for which they were seldom the worse, and sometimes such the better.

4. Other Officers

The balance between the civil and military elements aimed at by Lord in the construction of the Board itself was scrupulously observed also in the selection of those who were to work under it. Besides George Christian, the Secretary, upon John Lawrance had long fixed his eye, and Meelvil, who was specially appointed by Lord Dalhousie to the post of Assistant-Secretary. There were to be four Commissioners for the four divisions of the new province Lahore, Jhelum, Multan and Leia ; while beneath them again, come some fifty-two Deputy and Assistant Commissioners who were selected, in as nearly as possible equal numbers, from the civil and military services[1].

ACHIEVEMENTS OF THE BOARD

The machine of these three officers, so constituted and officially designated, a Board of Administration, consisted of Sir Henry Lawrence as President and the other two as members had each equal powers, and all three joint responsibility. There was no prospect that such a trinity would be opened indivisible, situation admirable suited to the taste of the interfering Dalhousie.[2]

But soon the administration began to suffer from the difference between the two Lawrence brothers, which came to a head over the questions of the treatment of the beneficiaries under the Sikh system. These ranged from the revenue assignees of many villages

1. You shall have, 'wrote Lord Dalhousie to Henry Lawrence, in anticipation of the annexation, on February 26, the best men in India to help you-your brothers John to begin with.'
2. Panjab Administration Report (1920-22), p. 24 Panjab under War & Peace Thorburn pp. 151-153, 190

to petty endowed institutions such as alms-houses and religious infant schools in villages. Dalhousie tried to ease the situation by appointing, in place of Mansel, "a delettante Philosopher," Robert Montgomery, the life-long friend of the brothers, to act as a sort of umpire between them.[1]

1. Pacification of the Panjab

The most difficult task before the Board was the pacification of the province. The greater portion of the Khalsa army which had made the British empire tremble at Ferozeshah and Chellian wala had frankly recognized the British supremacy, after the battle of Gujarat. They had thrown down swords in one vast pile, and had each, with one rupee, in his pocket returned to the plough. It was then the turn of few who had remained faithful during the struggle, obedient they mustered together with the armed retinues of the old Sikh nobility, at Lahore. The old and invalid among them were pensioned off. The remainder obtained their long arrears of pay, and permission was given, them of which they were eventually to avail themselves largely to re-enter the British service.

The reconciliation of the Sikhs to the new regime was due partly to the tactful handling of Henry Lawrence, but more to the political sagacity of the Sikhs themselves, "who had made up their minds to accept their defeat as final, and rise to wealth and honour a race, whose power and worth they had already learned to appreciate."[2]

2. General Disarmament

The Sikh army was disbanded. It remained to disarm the population and so to deprive them of the temptation to violent crime and disorder which the possession of arms always gave. Accordingly, about six weeks after annexation a proclamation ordering general disarmament was everywhere placarded, and was everywhere obeyed. 1,00,20,000 weapons of every size and every species, some of them much more dangerous to the wearer than to his

1. Montogomery his name to the District and town of Montgomery and the Montgomery Hall in Lahore.
2. Panjab under War & Peace-Thorburn, pp. 150, 159-161.

foe, ranging from the cannon or the rifle of the nineteenth century A. D., down to the quoit or the bows and arrows of the time of Porus and Alexander in the fourth century B. C., were voluntarily surrendered by the people of the province. The mountaineers of Hazara and of the Trans-Indus frontier were the only exception to the rule. They were allowed, and enjoined, to retain their arms ; for to have disarmed them at that early period would have been to render them a defenceless prey at the feet of their neighbours across the border[1].

3. Frontier Force Raised

The duty of protecting the Province which had thus deprived of the natural guardians af its peace fell on the British government. To guard the dangerous frontier line, it was arranged that ten regiments—five of cavalry and five of infantry should be raised from the Panjab itself. The people of various races—Hindustanis, the Sikhs, and Muslims responded cheerfully to the British call. The Sikhs, it had been feared by the government, might flock in dangerously large numbers against the British. The danger soon passed by. The Sikhs had rendered a valiant service whenever and wherever they were called upon to do so by the British Government. They had fought, with equal readiness, upon their own frontier and in other parts of India and abroad.[2]

A. The Irregular Regiments

Within a year several of the Panjab irregular regiments shed their blood in the British service, and henceforward they were seldom to shed it in any other cause. The Afridis, the Swattis, and other turbullent tribes beyond the frontier, learnt that their more peaceable neighbours had a formidable power behind them, which could not be provoked with impunity. They began to put some check on their predatory propensities. Three house field batteries, a camel corps stationed at Dera Ismail Khan and the famous Guide Corps, completed the movable defences of the frontier.[3]

---

1. Panjab under War & Peace-Thorburn. pp. 160-161.
2. Panjab Administration Report—1854, pp. 28-30.
3. Panjab Under War & Peace-Thorburn, p. 161.
   Panjab Administration Report—1851-52, & 1853, p. 37.

B. Guide Corps

But the 'Guide Corps' was a remarkable body of men. The corps owned its origin to a suggestion thrown out by the fertile brain of Sir Henry Lawrence at the close of the first Sikh-War. It originally consisted of only 250 men, horse and foot. But in view of the increased duties which were then to be thrown upon its numbers were to be trebbled. The Guide Corps contained on a small scale, representatives of almost every race and every place, every language and every religion, which was to be found in the North—and North-West of India. It contained men of every shade of moral-character, and men of no character at all.[1]

Recruitment to the Guide Corps

The cunning trackers, the notorious cattle-lifters, the daring freebooters, were enrolled in it. They were subjected to a whole-some discipline. They were clothed in a brown-uniform so as to be indistinguishable at a little distance from the ground on which they moved. They were further privileged to receive a high-rate of pay. Within a very short space of time they were found to be ready 'to go anywhere or do anything'. Endurance, courage, sagacity, local know-ledge, presence of mind, were the qualities which marked a man out for the Guide Corps.[2]

C. The Intelligence Department

On whatever point of the 500 miles of British Western Frontier, with its many savage tribes, operations had to be carried on. There were men amongst the Guides who could speak the language of a particular district, they had threaded before. Therefore, they could then thread again, its most dangerous defiles, and could tell where the hostile encampment or the robber-haunted cavern lay. Thus the Guides, formed the '*Intelligence Department of the Panjab.*' These were the men for a daring reconnaissance, for a forced march for a forlorn hope. Raised first by Lieutenant Harry Lumsden, they had already done good service in border fighting and in the Second Sikh-War. They were soon to serve under Sir Colin

1. Panjab Administration Report, 1851-52, & 53, p. 40.
   A Short History of British in India—Innes, pp. 291-92.
2. Panjab Administration Report, 1851-52, & 53, p. 40.

Campbell against the Mohmandas and their like, with unvarying success. Finally they were to be the first of that splendid succession of re-inforcement of which the Panjab was to denude itself in the day of peril.[1]

Measures to protect the Scientific Frontier of India

The whole Frontier Force described above, was made directly subordinate to the Board. It was placed under the command of Brigadier-General Hodgson. One portion of the frontier line was deemed by Lord Dalhousie to be of such paramount importance for the protection of the Empire that it was reserved for the regular troops. It was the Peshawar Valley, which-with the Khaibar Pass, the direct passage to Afghanistan, and thence into Central Asia, in its front. With the fords of the Indus, the best passage into India, directly in its rear,—was to be guarded by a force of about 10,000 men, nearly 3,000 of them Europeans. The Board had already shown by its measures that it was alive enough to take defensive measures.

It was thought that the dangerous parts, from Hazara to Dera Ismail Khan, should be defended by forts of considerable size, which were to be rendered capable of standing a siege. Below those, again, from the Tonk Valley down to Sindh, there should be a chain of smaller fortified posts at intervals of 12 miles apart. The whole should be connected together by a good military road, with branches leading, on one side, towards the hostile mountains, and on the others, towards the friendly river.[2]

So skilful and so complete were these defensive arrangements, that from time forward, the peace of the Panjab was never seriously threatened. The warlike preparations of the Board were thus all made, with a determination to stand firmly placed where they were against-all comers. The 'Wardens of the Marches,' chosen by the Lawrence for those posts of danger and difficulty, were great Generals.

Measures for Detection and Prevention of Crime

The next object of the Board was to provide for the detection

1. Settlement Mannual—James Douie, p. 14.
2. Panjab Administration Report, 1851-52, & 53, pp. 41-44.

and prevention of crime. To meet these ends, they raised two large bodies of police the one preventive, with a military organisation, the other detective. The preventive police were 8,000 in number, horse and foot, many among whom had done good service to the late Darbar, and had remained faithful to the British in the Second Sikh War.

The Military Preventive Police

The Military police was split in two sections the infantry, and the cavalry. Its final number was ten Battalions. The disbanded old soldiers of the Sikh Army, who remained faithful to the British during the Second Sikh War, were enlisted in the first of the four Battalions. "Each Battalion had a complete Indian complement of officers from the commanding officer[1] downward the whole force being under the supervision of four British officers, styled Police Captains." In addition to escort work for civil officers and treasure, and duty at the jails and other places they also assisted in garrison duty on the Frontier at such places as Kohat, Bannu and Hazara. Three of the Battalions were usually absorbed in the Leia Division being stationed in the Derajat.

The fifth Battalion was raised Rawalpindi by Lt. Miller, and did consistently a good work. Lt. Younghusband raised the sixth Battalion, which prominently shared in the military duties of the Frontier along with the Panjab Corps. In 1850, Captain R. Lawrence raised the seventh Battalion at Amritsar. "It was composed of a splendid body of young lads, sons of best yeomen of the Mahajan."[2] Sir John Lawrence remarked in the Administration report for 1852-53, that "in the force and vigour of its Police—the Panjab may challenge comparison with any province in India." "One Battalion—the sixth-volunteered for service in the Crimea and this Battalion as well as the third and the fifth made a contribution to the Patriotic Fund."[3] During the terrible outbreak of 1857, the Military Police were guarding Jails and Police Posts but in many

1. He was styled 'Komeidan (Commandant) a designation which was later commonly applied in some places to the Inspector of police.
2. A Brief History of Police Battalions H.L.O. Garret, p.2.
3. A Brief History of Police Battalions- H.L.O. Garret, p.3.

cases they were at once transferred to the Cantonments for regular military duty.[1]

The Detective Police

The other body numbering 7,000 men, and divided amongst some 230 police district (thanahs), was to be employed in the detection of crime, in the guarding of ferries, and in the collecting of supplies for troops or of boats for the passage of the rivers. "The Detective Police had to report crimes and track and arrest criminals. The serving of processes, the collection of supplies for troops and boats for the passage of rivers equally devolved upon them. They guarded ferries and often escorted Prisoners. A complete system of diaries and record was maintained."[2]

Large Powers to Tehsildars

With a wise trustfulness in its instruments, the Board left to the native revenue collectors, called tehsildars, large powers in the way of organising and controlling the police, thus utilizing the local knowledge which they alone possessed. The native village watchman, who formed an integral part of the old village system and was paid by the villagers themselves, was also carefully maintained by officers who had learnt the priceless value of the village communities in the North-West.[3]

Precautions for the Criminal Infested Districts

Special precautions were required in those districts which were more infested by criminals. The Peshawar-Valley for instance, was a nest of assassins, in which crimes of violence had always been the order of the day. Any hollow of the ground, gully, above all any tomb of a Muslim Saint, might, not improbably, harbour some desperate cutthroat. The centres of the Doabs, again, which were covered with jungle, or brushwood, or tracts of long grass, had been, from time immemorial a very sanctuary of cattle lifters and their spoil. In those natural fastnesses whole herds of oxen which had been driven off from the richer lands near the river might graze and wanter

1. A Brief History of Police Battalions-H.L.O. Garret, p.4.
2. A History of Development of the Police in the Panjab-B.R. Kalia, p. 17
3. Panjab Administration Report, 1151-52 & 53, pp. 92-93,

at pleasure, and yet lay impenetrably concealed former owners. The chance of finding his cattle would be small, and his chance of escaping with them with his life would be smaller still.

Peshawar & the Doabs

Round the city of Peshawar cardon behind cardon of police posts was thrown. They filled in the ravines and hollows and spread a network of roads over the adjoining districts. In the Doabs, which had never yet been crossed by anything but a camel track roads were laid in various directions, mounted patrols of police sent along them.

Professional Trackers were employed

Professional trackers were introduced men of whose amazing skill John Lawrence had again and again availed himself in the pursuit of criminals at Delhi, Panipat, and Gurgaon. They were men whose senses had been sharpened by natural or artificials selections of preter-natural degree of acuteness. They could discern a foot-print, invisible to the ordinary eye, in the hardest clay. They could follow a track of harried cattle through the wildest jungle and the roughest grass for, perhaps, some fifty-miles, naming before hand the number of the men and of the animals in the party, till at last they carried the trial triumphantly to some remote recampment, where their uncanny skill was proved to ocular demonstration[1].

Dacoity or Robbery

But cattle-stealing was by no means the worst crime with which the Board had to deal. Dacoity, or robbery in gangs, had been bound up with the whole course of Panjab history. The Sikhs had been cradled in it. It had grown with their growth. It was the most successful gang robber who, after winning by his trusty sword large quantities of money or of cattle, usually ended by carving out for himself, in much the same manner, broad estates or powerful principalities. The leader of a band was of free lances had thus little reason to be ashamed of his occupation. The districts of

1. Panjab Administration Report, 1858, pp. 14-17.
A History of the Development of the Police in the Panjab-B.R. Kalia. pp. 11-21

Lahore and Amritsar began to swarm with them. But strong precautions and wholesome severity soon checked the evil. During the first year thirty seven dacoits were condemned to death in Amritsar district alone ; in the second year the number fell to seven ; and in a few years more the crime ceased to exist throughout the Panjab.[1]

The Thaggi (Cheating)

There was more insidious crime, the existence of which seems at first to have been quite unsuspected in the Panjab. The prevalence of Thaggi in other parts of India had only been discovered in the Panjab also. Practices connected with it, the religious initiation, the patient plotting, the cool cruelty, the consummate skill and the professional enthusiasm of the culprits had given to it a world-wide celebrity.

A Dreadful Crime

The discovery of corpses by the side of wells or in the jungles after the dacoit had pretty well been exterminated, first aroused a suspicion that other confraternities of death might be found within the Panjab limits. Dead men tell no tales. No half-throttled traveller had ever escaped from their hands to tell the tale of the fellow-travellers. The 'Thag' had joined him on the road, had warmed themselves into his confidence. He often questioned him welfare, and, then, as he sat at food with them by the way-side, with one twist of the fatal handkerchief, attempted to give him a short shrift.[2]

The Panjab Thag was a mere bungler in his business. The fine art had been imported into the Panjab from India, and its first professor had been discovered and straightway hung up by Maharaja Ranjit Singh. His successors often made up for their want of skill in the use of the handkerchief by hacking their victim to pieces with their swords, and then, instead of pitching his body, still warm, into

---

1. A History of the Development of the Police in the Panjab—B.R. Kalia pp. 11-21
   Panjab Administration Report—1858, pp. 14-17
   Panjab Administration Report—1851-53, p. 50
2. Land of the Five Rivers—Trevaskis, pp. 103-215

the grave which they had opened while he was talking to them, they often carelessly left it to rot by the wayside.[1]

Thaggi Supressed

A Brahmin, who had been two-thirds strangled and left for dead, recovered and told his tale. The clue was followed up. Rewards were offered for the detection of Thag, a free pardon was promised to those who might turn Queen's evidence. A special officer was appointed for the investigation. A list of recent victims 264 in numbers was soon given in by approvers. A second list of professional Thags, given in by the same authorities, was published and posted everywhere.[2]

Many of them were apprehended altogether. The approver would often conduct the British Officer for miles.through the jungle without any apparent clue which could guide him in his search or refresh his memory. 'Dig here,' 'dig there,' he would say, as he came to a sudden stop in his tortuous course ; and the turning up for a few spadesful of soil revealed the corpse or the skeleton of one of his victims. Along one bit of by path 53 graves were thus opened and were all found to be tenanted.[3] The suppression of Dacoity and Thaggi was not a slight credit to the Panjab Administration Board, and not light gain to the cause of humanity.

Anti-Infanticide Movement

Since the period of the Board's Report (August 1852) a complete inquiry was made, in all the districts and divisions of the Panjab, as to the prevalence of the practice, which was found to extend to more places and to more tribes than had been previously supposed, especially to many sections of the Rajput tribe.

Prevalence of the Crime

It was ascertained that Hill Rajputs in the Cis-and Trans-Satluj

1. Panjab Administration Report—1858, pp. 9-14
2. A wonderful account is given in "Panjab Report (Selections from the Records of the Government of India No. IV),
3. One Thag was questioned as to the number of his victims. His professional pride was touched and with true enthusiasm he replied, 'How can I tell ? Do you remeber. Sahib every animal you have killed in the chase ? Thagi is our sport, our shikar (Dalhousie, Vol.I—Arnold, p. 259)

States, in the Bari Rechna and Chuj Doabs, the Bedis of Jullundur, Dehra Baba Nanak and Rawalpindi, the mercantile Khatris of the Mid Doabs from the Satluj to the Indus, the kingly Sadazais Pathans, the Mohmands tribes of the Multan Province, and the pastoral race on the banks of the Satluj and in the central wilds of the Panjab, were addicted to this inhuman custom. The whole province, with the exception of the Peshawar Division and the Trans-Indus Derajat, seemed to be in some degree infected with this social malady. The incentive was found to be two-fold : (1) Price of birth ; and (2) Price of purse ; that is, parents murder their infant daughters either because they could not afford the marriage expenditure which must one day be incurred on their account, or because they foresaw difficulties in marrying them suitably.

Measures Taken in the Trans-Satluj States

The first movements with a view to suppression were made in the Trans-Satluj States. Soon after the cession of that territory in 1847 proclamations were issued, depicting the enormity of the crime, and threatening the guilty parties with the consequences for murder. In 1852 meetings were held at which the representatives of the Bedis and Khatris tribes were convened and a lucid treatise on the causes, progress, extend and possible eradication of Infanticide was prepared by Major H.B. Edwards, then Deputy Commissioner of Jullundur.

Grand Meeting at Amritsar

At this important gathering all the nobility, chivalry and hierarchy of the old regime, and the wealth, rank and influence of the new, were assembled. The Sikh Sardars, the Hill Chieftains, the Commercial Millionaires, the Muslim Nawabs, the Hindu Pandits, were all invited. All the weight which official power and position could give was also added. There were present, in their public capacities, the Judicial and Financial Commissioners, the Commissioners of the Trans and Cis-Satluj States, and the District Officers of Ambala, Thanesar, Simla, Ferozepur, Ludhiana, Jullundur, Hoshiarpur, Kangra, Lahore, Amritsar, Sialkot, Gujranwala and Batala. Then the conclave of delegates of all the tribes and classes, assembled under a capacious awning, solemnly covenanted before the European Officers that they would prescribe, and cause the observance of, such rules regarding the intermarrying between various sub-divisions of the same tribe, and regarding the reduction of marriage expenses to a moderate scale, graduated for rich and poor, so that no man should feel any real difficulty in providing for his daughter in marriage, and should consequently have no motive for the commission of infanticide. The rules in question were fixed in detail by Committees, and were then published and proclaimed. The fame of this meeting spread far and wide throughout the Province, and the impression it created stood deep into the minds of the people.

Reformation of the Criminals

In dealing with the subject of crime, the Panjab Administration Board did not lose sight of the secondary object of punishment—the reformation of the criminals. Instead of being mutilated, or chained to a post in the streets, or placed at the bottom of a dry well like the methods of punishment of the system of Maharaja Ranjit Singh were subjected to a system of strict discipline and hard work, the Board brought reforms in the system. The criminals were decently clothed, fed and housed and were taught rudiments of education, and of a trade. Twenty-five Jails of different sizes and models, were erected in the different districts of the Panjab. The great central Jail at Lahore was built on the newest model with a view of economy and health, as well as the supervision, the classification, and the moral improvement of the prisoners. Thus John Lawrence was able, with the energetic help of Dr. Charles Hathaway, who was appointed Inspector of Prisons, to carry out the improvements in the system which he had long since indicated as desirable.[1]

THE LEGISLATION

Customs as the Basis of English Law

As regards legislations, the customs of the native were, taken as the basis of the law. A code of native customs was drawn up. Those customs which were absolutely bad and incapable of improvement were forbidden. Those which related to marriage, divorce, and tending to the degradation of the female sex, were first modified and then

1. Panjab Administration Report-1851-52 & 53, pp. 74-76.

accepted. Those which related to such subjects as inheritance and adoption were incorporated at once. The tahsildars, whose local knowledge marked them out as the best judges of local matters of small importance, were confirmed in their judicial as they had already been in their police authority. Each village, or group of adjoining villages, retained a court of its own, sanctioned by immemorial custom. Though the right of appeal to the Deputy Commissioner was reserved, yet a large portion of all matters in dispute could always be settled within its precincts.

The Land Tax

The land-tax was that varying share of the produce of the soil which was claimed by Government as its own. Under the earlier governments it was generally paid in kind. It was levied, harvest by harvest, by ill-paid officials, who were apt to take too little from the cultivator if he bribed them sufficiently, too much if he did not. In either case a large part of the amount, instead of finding its way into the coffers of the State, stopped short in the pocket of the tax-collectors. Under the system introduced by the English, a low average of the produce of a district was taken on the returns of several years together. The money value of the Government share was taken at another low average of current prices. All parties gained by this arrangement, but most of all the cultivator himself.[1]

Numerous land Tenures

The varieties of land tenure were numerous and complicated, but they were time-honoured. The Board in no case desired to destroy, but only to revive and to preserve them. The land-tax had in Maharaja Ranjit Singh's time amounted to half the gross produce, and had, generally been paid in kind. This payment in kind—not without strong protests on the part of the tax-payers was—abolished by the Board, and its amount reduced to half or to a quarter of what it had been before. Nor did the State suffer much by the remmission, for the revenues of Multan, which had become an integral part of the Panjab, and of other outlying parts, were flowing freely into the government treasury.[2]

1. Panjab Administration Report-1858, pp: 31-32
2. Panjab Administration Report-1858, pp. 32-34

Trade Policy Liberalised

On January 1, 1850 all town and transit dues, all export and import duties, were abolished by the Board. The preventive frontier line, 35 articles taxed by Mahraja Ranjit Singh was abolished. Trade was left free to flow in its natural channels. To balance these reductions, an excise, desirable in every point of view, was levied on spirits. Stamp duties were introduced, tolls at the chief ferries over the large rivers were authorised. A tax-necessary under the circumstances, but not theoratically free from objection, since it was laid on a necessity of life was imposed on salt. The vast stores of this mineral to be found in the Salt Range were henceforward to be managed by the British Government itself. To render the revenue accruing from it secure, the importation of salt from all neighbouring districts was prohibited. It was the one blot on an otherwise excellent fiscal system. But the people did not object to it, and found it no burden.[1]

The Public Works

The Public Works Department, in 1854, underwent a great change. Previously, the control of all Military Works in the Cis and Trans Satluj States, with the Military Board indirect subordination to the Government of India. The control of the Public Works in the Panjab proper and of the Defensive Works on the Trans-Indus Frontier, rested with a Civil Engineer immediately, subordinate to the Panjab Administration. But since 1854, all Engineering Works generally ; whether Civil, Military or Public had been placed under one Department, at the head of which was a Chief Engineer, and the supervision, financial and otherwise, over the whole, was entrusted to the Chief Commissioner.[2]

Napier, The Engineer

Colonel Napier had acted as Consulting Engineer to Sir Henry Lawrence during his Residency. He was well acquainted with its capabilities and its wants. He was a man of vast ideas, and had something in him of the 'greatsouled' man. If a thing was to be done well,

1. Panjab Administration Report-1851-52 & 53, pp.153-158
2. Panjab Administration Report-1858, pp. 21-32

and without a too close calculation of the cost, Napier was the man to do it. His ideas found expression in those splendid public works which are the pride of the Panjab, and are still a model for the rest of India.[1]

Roads & Canals

An efficient staff was placed at Napier's disposal. Lieutenant Alexander Taylor, was able to secure the warm affection of men so widely different from each other as Napier and Nicholson, as Sir Henry and John Lawrence. Funds fairly adequated to the occasion were placed at Mr. Napier's disposal, and special grants were to be made for work of imperial magnitude, such as the Grand Trunk Road and the great canals. Roads and canals are not made in a day and, in such matters, the work of the Board was, necessarily, one of preparation rather than of completion. During the first three years the progress of road buildings was as under :

1. 1,349 miles of road, had been cleared and constructed;
2. 853 miles were under construction;
3. 2,487 miles had been traced; and
4. 5,272 miles surveyed, and exclusive of minor cross and branch roads.

The Grand Trunk Road

During this period the G.T. Road had been traced, surveyed and put in progress. Operations on the chief obligatory points had been commenced ; however at that time no portion of the road had been opened. In a political and military point of view its consequence could hardly be over-rated, as binding together all the British great Northern cantonments and maintaining Communication with Peshawar, their greatest Frontier station, the most important place perhaps in that portion of Asia. In this respect it was a work not so much for this Province as for the Empire of India. But for the Panjab also it was of vast benefit as forming a great highway, passing through the upper districts and the chief cities, as commanding the entrance to Hazara, and giving access at several points to

1. Panjab Administration Report-1858, p. 46

Kashmir ; as constituting a great artery from which numerous branches separated in all directions. And lastly, it was the great outlet and channel for the land commerce and the import and export trade between India, Central Asia and the West. At that time (1851) it was contemplated to open speedily a road that might suffice for military exigencies.[1]

The Canals

The Mughals, who were magnificent in all they undertook, the Multan district had been intersected with canals. The native system, which compelled each village to pay its share of labour, towards keeping them in repair was found by Napier to be so fair and efficacious that he was content to 'leave well alone.' In the north of Bari Doab, a canal known as the Husli or Shah-i-nahar, 'the royal canal', had been carried from the point where the Ravi leaves the mountains—a distance of 110 miles—to Lahore. It was a grand work. But it fertilised no wastes and called into existence no villages. It simply supplied the royal water works, conservatories and fountains at the palace of Lahore.

Accordingly, another great work was proposed by the Board, which was as characteristics of the aims of the British Government in India as the Husli Canal had been of the natives. Starting from the same point in the Ravi, as though to emphasise the contrast a Canal was projected which, passing near the cities of Dinanagar, Batala, and Amritsar, should traverse the whole length ot the Bari Doab, should send forth from the upper part of its course, into districts which specially needed it, three branches, each of them from sixty to eighty miles long; should refill the empty reservoirs and the disused watercourses of the great southern waste, calling to existence everywhere new villages. Resusciating those which had fallen into decay, till, after a course of 247 miles, it joined the Ravi above Multan. The new canal would necessarily be the work of many years, but it was begun in faith, and was all but accomplished in the Chief Commissionership of John Lawrence.[2]

1. Panjab Administration Report. 1858, p. 47.
2. Panjab Administration Report, 1858, pp. 58-61.

The Currency

Naturally, the first thing which any conqueror did, was to strike off a coinage of his own. Thus it came about that in the Leia Division alone twenty-eight different coins were found to be in circulation, and that the rupee of Kashmir was worth barely two-thirds of that of the east India Company, while this last, again was inferior in purity and to the value of the old Nanak Shahi rupee, the symbol of the Sikh religion and power, which was coined at Amritsar and Lahore. Nor was this the worst ; for of the Nanak Shahi rupee itself there were not less than thirty varieties in circulation.

The commercial confusion, the illicit gains, the losses on exchange resulting from such a state of things could be imagined. All the illiterate classes must have suffered, and only the coiners, the money-changers, and possibly, the Sardars, would have thriven. Here was a case for prompt action to be taken by the British Government. The dead coinage were called in. They were sent to Bombay and Calcutta to be melted down and their equivalent was remitted to the Panjab, stamped with the mark of the English Queen. The coinage of the country was thus made to harmonise with accomplished facts, and within three years, three-fourths of the whole revenue paid into the British treasury was found to be in the British coins.

The Language Problem

The Languages of the Panjab were equally confusing. There was a sufficient variety of spoken languages. In the two western Doabs, Persian or dialects derived from it, were current ; in the eastern party Panjabi. In one of Indus districts, Pashto was spoken; in another Balochi. The difficulty of establishing a settled government and administering justice amidst these languages was great. An arrangement was ultimately reached that Urdu should be the official language of the eastern and Persian of the western half of the Panjab, and this compromise had been found to work well.[1]

1. Panjab Administration Report-1851-52 & 53, pp. 183-85.

Education

As regards education, the work of the first three years of the Board was chiefly preparatory. The first thing to be done was to ascertain what steps had been taken by natives in that direction. Robert Montgomery, is a name mentioned here for the first time in connection with the Panjab. Henceforward, almost as closely bound up with it as that of the Lawrences themselves—threw himself in the work with alarcrity. To his surprise and pleasure, it was discovered that throughout the Panjab there were elementary schools all for classes, Sikh, Muslim, and Hindu. The agricultural classes, unlike those of other parts of India, resorted to them in at least as large numbers as the higher castes, Rajputs, Brahmins or Khatries. More remarkable still, that even female education, which was quite unknown in other parts of the peninsula, was not altogether neglected.

In Lahore, for instance, there were sixteen schools for girls, with an average of six scholars in each, and what is still more noteworthy, all of them were Muslims. In fact, there was a general desire for education. The standard aimed at in those indingenous schools was, of course, not high. The stapple volume accepted by each creed, supplemented by a little writing and arithmetic—enough, at all events, to enable the Sikh to calculate his compound interest with accuracy, and to make him a good village accountant.

SUMMARY

The Board enjoyed wide powers and unrestricted control over all matters, pertaining to Panjab. The members wielded triple powers, civil, fiscal and criminal even to the extent of awarding death sentence and exercised general superintendence of every moral and material improvement of the annexed territory. The new administration was not encumbered with many regulations or tedious rules, which might be beyond the capacity of the people to understand or appreciate at that time. It was intended that the Panjab should be governed after "a ruder and simpler fashion."[1] Refined rules of procedure and complex technicalities were not suited to an ignorant people, little accustomed to written laws. The executive was composed "partly of

1. The History of the Administration of E.I. Company-Kay, p. 433

civilians and partly of soldiers, upon a mixed system into which the spirit of the Regulations was infused in such a manner as to cause it to harmonise and blend itself with all that was good in the spirit of native institutions."[1] It is to Dalhousie's credit that he unreservedly placed the most talented band of British officials—the flower of the service, at the Board's disposal the older provinces being denuded of such administrative calibre for the sake of the Panjab. Never was his skill better displayed as in his choice of agents for the Public Service in the Panjab.[2]

To each member of the Board was assigned a task, suited to his aptitudes and congenial to his genius. On Henry Lawrence devolved the political and military duties the disarming of the country, the demobilisation of the Khalsa army, the defence of the Frontier, the reorganisation of the new Panjabi and several other regiments.[3] He was to temper the cold winds of British Supremacy to the sect which was once dominant and powerful and still seething with indignation. He was to apply the balm and heal the wounds of all who would feel keenly the loss of their former powers and privileges. John who had already "achieved a high reputation as an administrator"[4] was to grapple with the intricacies of finance and land settlement.

The Board of Administration which governed the Panjab from April 1849 to January 1853, did precisely the work it was expected and meant to do. It accomplished what by unanimous verdict had been acclaimed "as a brilliant episode in British Indian annals.[5]" Maud Diver regarded the joint rule of Lawrences "unsurpassed for efficiency, unequalled for the rapidity and thoroughness with which a disorganised state was brought into order, an embittered and turbulent race turned into a loyal and contented population."[6] Sir Richard Temple goes further and says "The Board's operations were masterly in conception, thorough in foundation and business like in details. So far the

1. The History of the Administration of E.I. Company-Kay, p. 433
2. "Genius was not relegated to dull routine, nor dullness hoisted to positions of responsibility. The right men were drafted to the right places". (Edwin Arrold, Dalhousie's Administration of the British India, Vol. I. p. 352).
3. History of the Sepoy War, Vol. I-Kay, p. 52
4. History of the Sepoy War, Vol. I-Kay, p. 52
5. Men and Events of my Times in India-Temple, p. 65
6. Honouraria Lawrence-Driver, p. 373.

work had never been excelled and soldom rivalled in other provinces, either before or since that era."[1] Sir Charles Raikes was so impressed with the administrative results achieved by the Board, that he declared "The Panjab sysytem of government is so simple, so entirely developed to the genius of the people, that it must like truth, prevail, sooner or later over the entire peninsula."[2]

The most striking feature of the Board's work, perhaps was its comprehensiveness. Within less than four years, thousands of Ranjit Singhs' warriors were not only demobilised without any untoward incident but converted into peaceful and loyal subjects. It has been stated how the north Western Frontier was guarded and vigorous measures taken to maintain the internal peace. For the protection of the North West Frontier, a line of forts and cantonments, 500 miles in length was established, and to hold this line a new force called the Panjab Frontier Force, was created.

The entire judicial, fiscal and revenue systems of the province were reorganised and many reforms introduced under its paternal administration. the external face of the country was changed. Roads were built throughout the length and breadth of the province, and canals set a going which made the waste places blossom. "Peace hath her victories no less renowned than War."

The Board thus accomplished straight away, almost out of hand, with comparative completeness, that which others had done elsewhere by degrees. But the cardinal merit lay in this, that the Board did all those things simultaneously, in what was then regarded an incredibly short space of time. In order to form a correct estimate of the Board's work we must view it in the light of those days.

1. Men and Events of my Times in India-Temple, pp. 52-53
2. Notes on the Revolt in the N.W. Province of India-Charles, p. 171

3

Panjab Under John Lawrence (1853-1859)

The Board of Administration could not prolong enough. Sir Henry Lawrence was inclined to favour the Sardars, or Sikh aristocracy, who were devoted to him personally, and so pressed on with material improvements regardless of the cost to the revenue. On the other hand, John Lawrence had more sympathy with the peasants than the chieftains, and as guardian of the public purse brought forward many practical objections of his brother's pet schemes.[1]

The whole question took on a different colour when seen through the eyes of John Lawrence—the hard-headed administrator, unbiased by any such feeling for the Sikh Sardars. He regarded the Chiefs and Jagirdars as parasitic growths who lived on the blood of the honest ryot and put a heavy strain on the state exchequer. According to John Lawrence, the high dignitaries and feudal chiefs were a great hindrance in bringing the people in direct contact with the "benevolent British influence". John represented in his days the imperialism of Dalhousie. The gradual elimination of the princes and other intermediaries, and the establishment of direct British rule were the central features of the latter's policy. Besides his strong views on the elimination of Jagiradars, the question of finance influenced his mind.

Differences Between the brothers

The two brothers thus held strongly divergent opinions on this all important subject, which vitally affected the future of the Sikh aristocracy. After the dismemberment of the Sikh kingdom, it had

1. A History of British India-P.F. Roberts, p. 346

been Henry's ambition to secure for the Sikh Sardars and other functionaries of the Darbar an honourable position.[1] It was with a view to achieve this consummation that he had withdrawn his resignation of Residentship and consented to carry out the annexation policy of Dalhousie. When he saw that his brother was determined to thwart him in the policy he intended to pursue, all his pent-up anger came to the surface. On other questions like the mode of collecting land-tax or the plans to be followed in the Public Works Department, he had not felt so keenly and had been accommodating : but this was a point, intimately associated with all that he had lived and worked for, ever since he came in contact with the leaders of the Sikhs. To win liberal treatment for the vanquished, had been a predominant feature of Henry's schemes after the eclipse of the Sikh kingdom. John's insistence on the financial aspects of the question and his refusal to recognise the expediency of maintaining the remnants of the Sikh aristocracy, spelt the ruin of the class, Henry wished to preserve.

John appointed Chief Commissioner.

Nor till nearly three years had elapsed did these differences prove a serious bar to administration. But early in 1853, the two brothers mutually agreed that it would be better for one of them to go. Dalhousie believing, in spite of Henry's many good qualities, that John, 'take him all in all,' was the better man, removed the elder brother, to his deep chagrin, to Rajputana as an agent for the Governor-General. He abolished the Board that had served its purpose and made John Lawrence Chief Commissioner of the Panjab.

A Period of Peaceful Progress

The dissolution of the Board of Administration opened a new chapter in the eventful history of the Panjab. The period of transition from the Sikh to British rule was over. The brave and spirited people had been reconciled to the new order of the things. The disbanded Sikh soldiers quietly cast their "swords into plough-shares[2]". The foundations of a solid administrative structure had been laid. The grand projects calculated to ameliorate the condition of the masses had been launched. The roots of the British power had been dug fairly

---

1. Life of Sir Henry Lawrence-Edwards & Merivale, Vol, II, p. 176
2. Recreation of an Indian Officer-G.E. Malleson, p. 44

deep in the soil. Only vigilant attention and incessant labour were required to complete the fabric. John Lawrence, had then no complicate questions of policy to grapple with and no new problems or theory issues to tackle. No organic change was necessary anywhere and no new policies had to be initiated. The period under review therefore was essentially one of peaceful progress. No stirring events took place except at the end, when the Mutiny of 1857, shook the very foundations of British Indian authority. Then were tested the moulding skill and subduing energy of John Lawrence, as well as, the vitality of the structure he had consolidated during the four years.

Powers and Functions of the Chief Commissioner

John Lawrence inherited all the powers and functions hitherto vested in the Board of Administration.[1] His control over all departments and subordinate services was absolute and all-pervading. It included the defence and management of the whole trans-Indus frontier.[2] He was to be assisted by two Commissioners, who were to be assigned by Financial and Judicial branches of work respectively.

The new administration was not shackled with Regulations a'la Cornwallis. The Judicial system as initiated by the Board was maintained. Further, no elaborate rules were prescribed for the guidance of the Chief Commissioner. 'The Panjab was to be governed by a strong hand, unfettered by the tedious regulations. Responsibility was undivided, and the delegation of power went down in an unbroken chain of subordination. The result was that all the scattered threads met in one hand which could relax or tighten the grip as he thought fit.

REFORMS OF JOHN LAWRENCE

Panjab Divided into Divisions, Districts and Tahsils

The province was divided into seven divisions.[3] Each division in turn was subdivided into small districts, so that intimate contact

1. Political Consultation, February 4, 1853 No. 129/Foreign Department, I.R.D.
2. The District of Peshawar excepted.
3. (1) Cis-Satluj States Division (2) Trans-Satluj States Division. (3) Lahore. (4) Jhelum (5) Multan. (6) Leia. (7) Peshawar. (The Panjab Administration Reports, 1858, p. 4)

between the people and the Deputy Commissioners was practicable.[1] Each district was further divided into tahsils under Tahsildars. But of these units the really vital one was the district which was for most purposes a practically independent political unit, of which the Deputy Commissioner was the benevolent despot. The province started on its career with a splended set of administration, half of them picked civilians from the North-Western Provinces. the others selected military men who preferred the pay and power of administrative work to routinism in regiment.[2]

Offlcers To Move Among The People

The district officers were instructed to move among the people and cultivate personal contacts with all classes, so as "to banish all sense of strangeness from their minds, and to make them feel at home under the British rule."[3] John Lawrence abhorred the idea of British Officers living on olympian heights, cut off from the main currents of popular feeling.

The Deputy Commissioners and their assistants, so, Kay tells us, "were Judges, revenue collectors, their catches diplomatists, conservancy officers, and some times sergeant and chaplains, all in one.[4]" The multifarious duties, they performed, involved, chncentration of enormous power in their hands. It will not be incorrect to say that those officers were dictators in miniature. But their dictatorial sway had two redeeming features—confidence and paternalism. "They had, a respect for native ways and institutions and did not consider a thing bad because it was not English. They put themselves in the people's place and made the interests and the care of the people their own, striving to identify them with the Government, and create as it were a family feeling.[5]" This intimate relationship yielded rich dividends during the Mutiny of 1857.

1. Lord Lawrence-Aitcheson, pp. 60-61
2. Land of the Five Rivers—Trevarskis, p. 156
   Panjab Administration Reports-1858, p. 24
   The Land System of British India-Baden Powell, Vol. II. p. 728
   India as I knew it—O'Dwyer, p. 28
3. Men and Events of my Times in India-Temple, p. 57
4. History of the Sepoy War, Vol. I-Kay, p. 55
5. Lord Lawrence-Aitcheson, p. 69.

Period of Successful Development

The change in the constitution of the Government—a chief with two subordinate heads of departments, one financial, the other judicial, replacing a co-equal triumvirate—took place on abolishing the Board of Administration. The concentration of power in the hands of one man facilitated the rapid disposal of business. John Lawrence's habit was to have no arrears, to clear his official basket daily. This he did until on May 12, 1857, the fateful telegram from Delhi, announcing the seizure of the city by the Meerut mutineers. It had diverted his energies from the routine of peaceful administration to the stern necessities of a struggle for life and empire. During the preceding four years the history of the province was comprised in two words—successful development.'' Whatever the Board had begun, the Chief Commissioner had vigorously continued.[1]

North-West Frontier Policy

The North-Western Frontier of India with its rugged regions and fierce and freedom-loving people claimed the constant attention of John Lawrence. It was the same old question of curbing the trans-frontier tribes in their predatory habits. The Guide Corps and the Panjab Frontier Force could not permanently stop the tribal raids. For centuries the Pathan and Baloch tribes had grown accustomed to take toll from the trade routes and to make frequent inroads into the plains.

Lord Dalhousie had no wish to extend the boundaries of the Panjab, beyond the line of the Sikh conquest and invite a perpetual headache. He maintained the status quo and respected the independence of the trans-frontier tracts. No intervention was accompanied by conciliatory gestures like grants of land and allowances.[2] But the Pathan temper was incorrigible. The tribes men soon proved to be dangerous.[3]

---

1. History of India-Vol. I-Trotter, pp. 193-194.
   Directions of Revenue Officers in the Panjab-Barkley, p. 25.
2. Lord Lawrence-Temple p. 82
3. Lord Lawrence-Temple, p. 80.

TWO DIFFERENT LINES OF POLICY

A. The Tribal Belt should be Annexed to the Panjab

B. Non-Intervention of Tribal Affairs.

To deal with the tribes effectively, two different lines of policy were suggested at that time. The one recommended that the tribal belt should be annexed to the Panjab and the frontier be extended beyond the old Sikh boundary. This was the 'forward' school of thought. This school dreamt of trans-Khaibar conquests. They advocated that the British Indian Empire should possess a sound strategic frontier and this frontier could be founded in Afghanistan. Like Lord Lytton, it "painted a fancy prospect of...bequething to India the supremacy of Central Asia and the revenues of a first-class power."[1]

The other school advocated non-intervention in tribal affairs but suggested strong measures on the Indus frontier. The latter considered that the block of mountains, the inhospitable nature of the trans-frontier territory and the ferocious tribesmen formed a difficult and effective barrier against Russia. John Lawrence and Herbert Edwardes belonged to the second school of thought. As John Lawrence's Government had no intention of permanently occupying the Pathan territory, military action—necessarily took the form of a punitive expedition followed by a withdrawal. The object was to convince the tribes by some direct action that the armed incursions into the plains and attacks on Government personnel harmed their own cause and jeopardised their own interests which could be best served by peaceful behaviour.

John Lawrence did not wholly rely on force to preserve the border peace. He maintained the conciliatory method of the Board. Their allowances, subsidies and grants of land, all were confirmed.[2]

Crimes Suppressed

Reviewing in 1856 each branch of his administration John Lawrence recorded with satisfaction "the attachment of the people to their own fude jury system was unabated ; crime was mild and rare, and on

1. Letter to Sir James Stephen, April 7, 1880. Printed in Lady Betty Balfour's Lord Lytton's Indian Administration, p. 422.
2. The Second Panjab Administration Report, p. 12.

its occurrence was rigorously prosecuted and condignly punished ; a considerable number of Thags—a robber fraternity of highway pioso-ners and stranglers—400 were still at large ; but their devices were utterly confounded, and they found themselves so tracked that they could not commit crimes. The convict population had risen to 12,000, but institution ; besides seven Government schools, of a superior kind, and eight good missionary schools, there were in all 3372 indigenous or village schools, as yet of the rudest description.

EDUCATION

1. Early system of Education was Primitive

The early system of education was most primitive. The teachers derived a precarious subsistence from fees. There were no funds available for popular education. In reality, children were hardly receiving any good education. The schools referred to being merely infant rote—schools sort of religious kindergartens, in which the prattlers repeated in Gurmukhi, Hindi, Arabic, o Persian sentences from their several scriptures. As a leaven to operate upon this mass of ignorance, Lawrence wrote that he had arranged to open 30 schools at district headquarters, 100 village schools in rural tracts, four normal schools and a central college at Lahore, the whole to be supervised by one director and two inspector of schools, and the cost to be £ 30,000 plus £ 1500 as grants in-aid to missionary and other private schools.

2. John introduced the System of Teaching of Elements of English Education

His declared object was that, the mass of the people be taught the plain elements of English knowledge in their own language. The funds for the purpose were to be obtained from the people themselves by one per cent education cess on the revenue. Had John Lawrence foreseen that the peasantry would not send their sons to schools, but that the village money-lenders and traders would, it was certain that he would not have taxed the peasants for the benefit of the money lender's community, yet such had been the case throughout 75 per cent of the villages of the Panjab during the half century that had elapsed since popular education was inaugrated.[1]

3. Vernaculars were made the Mediums of Instructions

The beginning which John Lawrence made in the direction of imparting education was by way of making the schools popular and fixing vernaculars the medium of instruction. The introduction of English in the early stages would have rendered the whole scheme unpopular and defeated its own purpose, at the very outset. Besides the Government schools situated in the District Headquarters and in the interior, the Lawrence Administration's active measures to encourage both the urban and rural people to set up schools in their own areas were to be aided and supervised by Government.[2]

LAND-TAX

1. Shree Quarters of the State Sources

In his review the Chief Commissioner naturally dwelt at length on his favourite subjects, the "land-tax" or the land revenue and the condition and prospects of the agriculturists. "When it was remembered", he wrote "that this tax (land revenue) furnished three-quarters of the state resources, that was paid by agriculturists comprising three-quarters of the population, that their contentment and happiness was more vitally affected by the manner in which that tax was levied and administered than by any circumstances whatsoever, the extreme importance of the subject was manifest." Discussing his share in the surrender of revenue in the first summary settlement made after annexation, he asserted that "on the whole the reduction of taxation allowed by the British Government on its first occupation of the country was not less than fifty lakhs,[3] at the lowest.

2. Peasantry Largely Benefited

In the calculation, John Lawrence allowed nothing for bad reasons, cattle disease, deductions from the threshing-floor heap

1. Dalhousie's Administration of British India, Vol. I. Arnold, pp. 279-80. Panjab Administration Report, 1858, pp. 55-56.
2. The Punjab Administration Report, 1851-53, p. 44.
3. Or £ 500,000 sterling.

for village services, interest on debts, and the like. Answering the charge made by Sikh Sardars and others, that, in his desire to benefit the cultivators, he had sacrificed income to which Landlords and Jagirdars were entitled. He said that the allegation was true, and that extreme moderation in assessments had been necessary to ensure peasant prosperity. He then demonstrated by figures that by lapses of fiefs and resumption of Jagirs-the point on which he and his brother had differed, and which Lord Dalhousie had decided in his favour—he had recouped to the state all that he had given up for the good of the people.

3. A Light-Tax Due to Fall in the Prices

John Lawrence further explained that his policy "to tax lightly the agriculturists" had been partly due to the more or less permanent fall in prices of "50% nearly" since annexation ; but a simple sum in proportion showed that, if, when cash assessments were first imposed, the commutation prices were 50 per cent higher than they subsequently ruled, the reduction made between 1852-56 were incommensurate with the fall in prices.

4. Agriculture Being the Sole Occupation of the People

Discussing prospects he expected agriculture to remain the sole occupation of Panjabis, and that without facilities for export "there must always be some anxiety regarding land revenue. "Let means of export, the grand desideratum, be once supplied, everything will follow." To supply the peasantry with an outlet for their surplus produce, estimated by him was at 777,481 tons annually. He pushed on roadmaking in all the Doabs, and convinced that "the valley of the Indus must become the great highway for the export trade of the Panjab. That upon that trade more than upon any other circumstance the entire future of the province will depend. He promoted the extension of that costly failure "the Indus Steam Flotila" to Makkhad, north of Kalabagh.

5. Non-Agriculturists Were also Benefited

That non-agriculturists capitalised, after reducing a large part of the peasant proprietory to the condition of villeins, might some day be the only class to share with the Government all the profits of the grain trade, was a contingency which never occurred to him. Whilst admitting that the British system of administration was beneficial to village money-lenders, and "enhanced facilities for recovering their loans from the landholders", he maintained that "on the other hand the proprietory bodies were becoming less and less dependent on them, as frugality, prudence and good management increased under the influence of the money-payment system."

The condition showed that John Lawrence's faith in his peasantry and "money-payment system" was misplaced, and that he wholly misapprehended the effects of fixed cash assessments, uncertain harvests, and the possession of credit plus freedom of contract and an up-to date legal system.

6. Remissions of Land Tax were Granted

However, three-fourths of the population of the Panjab were engaged in agriculture. The change from grain payment to money payment had continued to cause widespread distress to the cultivators who were unable to pay even the reduced land-tax. The continuance of low-prices, added to their misery. To meet the situation without changing money economy remissions of land-tax were granted. To safeguard the interests of the peasant proprietors, their holdings were registered and their rights recorded.[1] The defects, such as waste of manure, the exhaustion of the soil caused by faulty rotation of crops, the injudicious methods of planting seeds were all impressed upon the peasants.[2] The low price level made it difficult for the agriculturists to secure money, with which to pay their taxes.

JUDICIAL ADMINISTRATION

1. Small Courts Popular with the People

Justice was further improved by bringing it nearer to the peasant's door by means of small Cause Courts, started all over

1. The Second Panjab Administration Report, p. 192
2. The Third Panjab Administration Report, p. 6,
The Fourth Panjab Administration Report, p. 7

the province. There were in all 104 such courts, besides 11 regular Court. The Small Causes Courts became very popular with the people. About two-thirds of the judicial business was conducted in these Courts. These were so situated as to eliminate long journeys of over 14 miles on the part of suitors, who could return to their homes by the evening after attending to their cases.

2. The Procedure was Very Quick

The procedure laid down was as quick and simple as in the Central Courts. The average duration of a suit in 1854 was twenty-eight days and in 1855 even this was reduced to twenty-three days. No fees were charged by the Courts for professional advice given to the people. The employment of pleaders was very rare and every effort was made by the Administration to discourage it. The people flocked to officers who presided over them.

3. Gained Good Will of the People

The efficiency, impartiality and promptness displayed by the Courts did much to help the administration to gain popular good-will. They, who in 1849 had a dislike for the English and had staked their all to drive them, became the main prop of their regime in 857 A.D.

THE CENSUS

The Census was taken during the night of December 31, 1854, with the acquiescence and even ready help of the people themselves, a fact proving the confidence and good understanding existing between the subjects and the Government. The population of British possessions in the Panjab was found to be nearly thirteen millions about three millions, in excess of the rough guesses of 1849.

Its density ranged from 334 a square mile in the richest districts in the Manjha, about Lahore, Amritsar and Jullundur, to 62 in the Muslim tracts west and south of Lahore. The number of villages was returned as 26,000; the cities with populations exceeding 50,000 were four—Amritsar, 122,000; Lahore,

94,000; Multan, 56,000; Peshawar, 53,000. Of the total population seven and a half millions were Muslims and five and a half Hindus. The Sikhs were every-where classsed as Hindus, except in the Lahore division, in which they were most numerous and separately counted. In that division they were returned as 2,00,000 only, out of a population of three millions. The smallness of the total was accounted for by the supposition that, as the Sikhs militant commonwealth had been destroyed, their children were no longer initiated, and were consequently regarded as Hindus.

Extension of Telegraph System

The extension of the telegraph system to the Panjab, was specially noteworthy, as through its agency the authorities were forewarned of the seizure of Delhi by the Meerut mutineers, and enabled to take timely measures to disarm sepoy regiments before their plans were ripe for execution. To Lord Dalhousie goes the credit of introducing and energetically pushing telegraphy in India. By 1857 he had given the country 4000 miles of instanttaneous communications, including an excellently equipped line. from Calcutta to Peshawar. At that time Indians still believed, the sending of messages by wire to be devilish witchcraft, and preferred runners to trained lightning. Thus the Government was everywhere in a position to carry out its plans for self-preservation days.[1]

THE MUTINY

At Meerut on May 10, 1857 A.D. when the station was plunged in the calm of Sunday evening, three Indian Regiments rose, shot dead their officers, broke open the prisons and released their comrades. The telegram from Delhi was received by John Lawrence on May 11, 1857 at Rawalpindi, that "the sepoys from Meerut have come in and are burning everything—Mr. Todd is dead, and, we hear, several Europeans—we must shut up.[2]" "His (John Lawrence) practical mind at once grasped the extent of the peril—

1. Panjab Administration Report, 1858, pp. 67-69
2. The Panjab and Delhi in 1857, Vol. I-Browne, p. 91

the imminent mutiny of the Bengal army—and the means by which it should be overcome. His parochialism had been that of the devoted local officer, not as the cramped understanding ; on the instant it overleapt its provincial walls and included all India.[1]"

At that time the Panjab was garrisoned by 59,656 troops of whom 35,900 were sepoys, whose sympathies lay with their rebellious brethern. Of the remaining 25,756 troops, 10,326 were Europeans and the rest were the Panjab Irregulars.[2] Out of twelve regiments, seven were cantoned, on the Simla Hills or in the Peshawar Valley. Thus there were five regiments stationed at Ferozepore, Lahore, Sialkot, Jullundur and Rawalpindi.

MILITARY POSITION

1. **Panjab Was Administered through non-Panjabi officials**
2. **Military position was not very sound.**

Most of the vital military centres like Attock, Kangra, Phillaur were held by the Hindustani troops.[3] The province having been recently conquered, its inhabitants were not yet wholly trusted by the government. It was, therefore, held in subjugation by a large proportion of the sepoys, while the revenues were collected and the laws administered in the great measure through the medium of non-Panjabi Officials.[4] Thus it would appear that from the military point of view the position of the Panjab was not very reassuring. There was a danger that the European troops might be overwhelmed by the sepoys who held most of the magazines and arsenals. There was, however, one relieving feature ; there existed a deep antagonism between the non-Panjabi troops and the Panjabis.[5] The people and soldiery of this province regarded the sepoys as an army of occupation, and detested them even since the first Sikh war.

1. Panjab Under War & Peace-Thorburn, p. 188,
2. The Mutiny Reports, Volume VIII, Part II, p. 328.
3. The Mutiny Reports, Volume VIII, Part II. p. 328
4. The Mutiny Reports, Volume VIII, Part I. p. 228
5. The Mutiny Reports, Volume VIII, Part II, p. 359

POLITICAL POSITION

1. The Punjab was Well Protected

Politically, the Panjab was well protected. All influential Sardars who "might have become the centres of disaffection"[1] were either exiled or had died by that time. There was no nucleus left round which the anti-British elements might gather. The new landed aristocracy was enjoying solid benefits under the new regime and had no wish to exchange security for anarchy, the terror of which was still surviving in the recollections of the people. In the absence of any agitators or popular leaders, the masses were pathetic. "To the great bulk of the rural population, echoes, of the life and death struggle going on before Delhi, were as void of personal interest as is the roar of breakers to the inmates of snug quarters some distance from sea.[2]"

Moreover, a succession of abundant harvests had put them into good humour. Trade was flourishing and there was general comfort and prosperity everywhere.[3] The people had no particular grievance and hence there was no desire for change.[4] The paternal administration of John Lawrence had won their confidence and disarmed their fears for the future. There was also a general feeling among all classes that no force in India could ultimately prevail against the English organisation and resources. Thus the Mutiny could not have been more timely for the effective demonstration of the Panjab loyalty to the British cause.

EXTERNAL POSITION

Externally too, the Panjab had no fear of any invasion, Afghanistan under Dost Muhammad Khan was a friendly power and was greatly indebted to the British Government for the material aid it had rendered in fighting the Persian menace. The trans-Indus tribes had been over-awed by military expeditions and for 'one crime or another almost every powerful tribe beyond

---

1. The Fourth Panjab Administration Report (1856-1858), para 149
2. The Panjab in Peace and War-Thournburn, p. 211.
3. The Fourth Panjab Administration Report, para 149.
4. The Fourth Panjab Administration Report, Para 149

the border was under a blockade.[1] The turbulent districts of Kohat and Hazara had been "tamed by easy revenue and kindly rule."[2] In the valley of Peshawar the same ease and prosperity prevailed which the other parts of the province enjoyed. The Panjab Frontier Force was in high spirits.[3] Every important post on the Frontier was filled by a capable man. Such in brief was the state of the North-West Frontier when John Lawrence was telegraphically informed, that the insurgents had taken possession of Delhi.

REASONS FOR JOHN'S SUCCESS

1. A good bumper harvest

2. Panjab army equipped with superior weapons.

3. The Indus frontier was garrisoned with local forces

4. Afghanistan friendly with the British Government

The Panjab had, for the third time in succession a good bumper harvest. The people were in a very happy frame of mind. Its interior cantonements held the bulk of the British troops who had served in Bengal, most of them armed with the new Enfield, rifle, a weapon crushingly superior to the "gas-pipe" Brown Bess of the mutineers. In addition the Panjab's Indus frontier was garrisoned by the lately trained provincial army men, heartily loyal and keen for active service for the British in any part of the world. Further, Persia was willing to surrender Herat to the Amir of Kabul, and was allowing him a subsidy of £ 220,000 a year. He and his Afghan subjects for the first time in Anglo-Indian history, were friendly towards the British Government.

5. Unpopularity of the Purbias

Thus, the Mutiny of the Bengal army occurred at an opportune time for the effective demonstration of Panjab loyalty. The mutineers also could not remove more likely to unite the people of this province. In addition to the prospect of sacking Delhi, the Sikhs had recent scores to pay off their narrow defeats by the English, had been honourable to the vanquished. The Purbias, who

1. The Mutiny Reports, Volume VIII, Part II, p. 132
2. The Mutiny Reports, Volume VIII, Part II, p. 132
3. Lord Lawrence-Richard Temple, p. 89

had run away in battle, formed two-thirds of the garrison of the Panjab. They boasted that they, not the English, had humbled the pride of the Khalsa and were holding them down. This was a bitterness to swallow for a domineering people, who but for the English, would have long before placed their Maharaja on the Peacock throne of the effete Mughal.

6. Bitterness of the Sikhs against the Hindustanis

The Sikhs had remembered with bitterness that they had lost their independence through the evil counsels of the Hindustanis in their service—fact borne out by Sir Henry Lawrence himself, who, writing in 1856 of the causes of Anglo-Sikh wars, had said : "Proportionately few of the instigators of opposition at Lahore in the Sikh Army were Sikhs. They were mostly British subjects, many of them British deserters. The general feeling of the Sikhs was hardly hostile ; many of the Sikhs were friendly, decidedly so, compared with the Hindustanis in the Panjab service," and since those wars, not only was the Sikh fatherland garrisoned by those, but every civil post of emolument was held by Hindustanis, Sikhs, and indeed all Panjabis, had therefore in 1857 good cause to side with British government."

JOHN LAWRENCE AND THE MUTINY

Strict Measures Taken

During the first forty-eight hours after the receipt of the news from Delhi, John Lawrence at Rawalpindi and Robert Montgomery, the judicial Commissioner, at Lahore, a man as resolute and during as his Chief, acted independently, for telegraphic communication between the two stations was interrupted. They forestalled a local mutiny by asking the military authorities to disarm Bengal regiments, wherever possible. Before the news of the fall of Delhi could be known strict measures were had beeh taken by John Lawrence. This military action was rendered more effectively by the subsidiary measures taken by the civil authorities to prevent the possible spread of disaffection.[1]

1. Panjab Under War & Peace-Thorburn, pp. 198, 227-8.
A Short history of the British in India-Innes, pp. 314-315,

1. Civil Officers to Punish Summarily

Civil officers were immediately empowered to try and punish summarily, even with death, offences affecting the public tranquility.

2. Strict Censorship was Maintained

A strict but judicious censorship was maintained over the native press. All letters addressed to sepoys were opened, and much curious and valuable information was thereby obtained. All treasure was concentrated at places where a European guard could be obtained.

3. Ferries All Over The Rivers were Guarded

The ferries over the five great rivers of the Panjab were guarded with special care and the country was thus divided into blocks of territory insulated from each other. All Hindustanis without employment were deported out of the Panjab and mendicants and roving faqirs coming from the east were turned back.

Attitude Of The Money-Lending Class

But while the rural population eagerly co-operated in the enforcement of these measures, the attitude of the money-lending classes their loyalty was only 'secured' by the exaction of a forced loan. This loan served to ease the financial difficulties which the province experienced in meeting a heavy military expenditure, at a time when all remittance from Calcutta were cut off and it took some time for money from Bombay to reach Lahore. Disorders were kept in check by fining the persons, villages or towns implicated in them, to the amount of the property plundered.

Rewards For The Co-operation of The People

The active co-operation of the people in the extirpation of the mutineers was secured by paying a reward of Rs.50 for every mutinous sepoy delivered up alive, the captors being permitted to retain any property found on the sepoy's person. The effect of this order was to place the Hindustanis as soon as they left cantonment among people who stood to gain by handing them over. These measures sufficed for the security of the Province as a whole, though local outbreaks in the hills of the north-west and amongst the pastoral tribes in the jungles between Lahore and Multan showed the danger, that the Goverment might have had to face had it show any signs of weakness.[1]

Native Regiments Disarmed at Mianmir

Montgomery lost no time to take immediate action : that wired warning gave its possessors several days' advantage over their undeclared enemies : telegram in hand he rose to Mianmir and easily converted Brigadier Gorbett to his views. "An intelligent Sikh, a non-commissioned officer in the Police Corps, had discovered that a deeplaid conspiracy had been formed by the Mianmir native troops, which involved the safety of the fort of Lahore, and the lives of all the European residents in the cantonments and civil station of Anarkali.[2] After the annexation of the Panjab, all the forces were stationed at Anarkali, but later in 1851, 52, the troops were moved to Mianmir, situated 3 miles to the east of Lahore on account of the unhealthiness of the Anarkali area. The cantonment then stood on an arid plain, originally bare of trees.

A ball was being given that night to the officers of her Majesty's 81st Foot, the only British regiment in the station, and for the following morning a general parade had already been ordered. To lull suspicion no change of programme was made, except that just before moving to the parade-ground the guns of the two batteries of horse artillery in garrison were loaded with grape, balled ammunition was served out to the 81st and three of its companies were marched off to Lahore.

When the parade began, the three native infantry regiments and one irregular-cavalry regiment, were brought up face to face with the remaining five companies of the 81st, who at once opened out, disclosing twelve guns with port-fires held lighted, in readiness for immediate action. Before the astonished sepoys and troopers had grasped the full meaning of the manoeuvre, the words of command, "81st, load." were ordered. Amazed and cowed, all four regiments' as soon as ordered to pile arms, did so after a momentary hesitation thus in a few minutes

1. Panjab under War and Peace-Thorburn, pp. 212-213.
   Imperial Gazetteer of India, p. 35.
2. The Panjab & Delhi in 1857 Vol, I Browne, pp. 93-94.

over three thousand probable mutineers were renderd weaponless, and impotent for mischief.[1]

This initiative on the part of the British Officers was so swift, so bold in design and execution that the Maliks and their followers, who witnessed the scene, were completely taken aback. The vigours of the proceedings impressed the Panjab Chiefs, who soon after the parade, flocked in and expressed their eagerness to carry out the commands of the Government.

Gobindgarh (Amritsar)

Originally this fort-belonged to Sardar Gujar Singh Bhangi, but was rebuilt by Maharaja Ranjit Singh. It was made the repository of the Maharaja's treasures, and was garrisoned by 2000 troops and had 20 guns of large calibre mounted upon its ramparts.

Scarcely less important than the fort at Lahore was that of Gobindgarh at Amritsar. Its real value did not consist in its occupying any commanding position in a military point of view, or in containing any arsenal like Phillaur and Ferozepore, nor in its strength of construction, but in its national religious character. The possession of it, like the possession of the famed Kohi-noor, carried with it the *talsmanic* pledge of power. If this fort, sacred from its proximity to Sikh holy city, named after Guru Govind Singh, and rich in traditions and relics of the Sikh race and faith, had once been wrested from the British hands, the prestige of the government would have been imperilled.

The British force in the fort and the adjacent cantonment at that time was small. One Company of European artillery, under Captain Macleod, occupied the fort, the guard being supplied by a detachment of the 59th N.I. from the station, where also was a company of foot-artillery (native), and a light field-battery. The company of H.M. 81st despatched by the brigadier from Lahore, the previous day in *ekkas* under Captain Chichester, entered the fort before day light, accomplishing the intervening thirty miles in a single night ; and for its greater security, the company of European artillery destined for Phillaur was detained by the Amritsar authorities. As soon as the outbreak

1. Mutiny Correspondence-Vol VII Part I. p. 64.
2. Mutiny Correspondence-Vol. VIII Part. II p. 136.

occurred, one of the first measures adopted by the.Deputy Commissioner, Mr. Cooper, was to Provision this fort. It was rapidly and the roughly affected without exciting any particular notice, and the fort then became the safest bulwarks for the protection of Europeans of this District.[1]

Ferozepur Arsenal

At a court of inquiry assembled some time previous to the Delhi mutiny, a Native Officer of the 57th Native Infantry at Ferozepur declared that it was the purpose of his regiment to refuse the Enfield cartridge if preferred to them. This raised a strong feeling of suspicion against the Corpos, but the 45th Native Infantry, which was not on good terms with the 57th and had openly declared their contempt of the 57th, was considered staunch. On the 14th May, as soon as newes by express from Lahore of the Delhi disaster reached Brigadier Innes, who had on the previous day taken command, ordered the entrenched arsenal to be immediately garrisoned by part of Her Majesty's 61st Foot and the Artillery. All Ladies were also removed thither, and the two regiments of Native Infantry ordered into camp in positions of about three miles apart.[2]

The way of the 45th Native Infantry lay past the entrenchment. As they approached, their column insensibly swered towards the glacis. The movement had barely been observed when they swarmed up the slope and attacked the position. The Europeans in an instant divined their intent, and rushed to the ramparts with the bayonet. The attack was repulsed ; but before the 61st could load, the sepoys dashed at the gate, whence they were also flung back, and then with an air of injured innocence they reformed their column and marched quietly with their European officers to the camp.

During the night the church, the Roman Catholic chapel, the school-house, 17 officers' houses and other buildings were burnt to the ground by the men of the 45th. On the 14th the treasury was moved into the entrenchment, and it was discovered that of the 45th Regiment there only remained 133 men ; the rest, with large part of

1. Amritsar District Gazetteer, p. 22.
2. Ferozepur District Gazetteer, p. 41

the 57th, had deserted. The remaining portions of these regiments were subsequently disbanded.[1]

Unfortunately the brigadier was one of the many incompetents whom the seniority system had raised to responsible position. Had he followed the advice wired to him from Lahore, arsenal and cantonment would have been by the morning of the 13th May as securely British as were Mianmir and Lahore fort. Instead of acting vigorously he had Her Majesty's 61st Foot and some gunshe pottered and harangued. He sent a company of the 61st to garrison the arsenal, but he neither disarmed not turned out the wing of the 45th Native Infantry, who had been in sole charge of the place. He paraded the regiment and spoke like a father to the sepoys, and forthwith helped by their comrades inside the arsenal, they attempted to rush upon the British guards and not until another company of the 61st was hurried up did the scrimmage cease.[2]

Had the mutineers been at once followed and annihilated, the matter would have ended. Instead, Innes adopted a defensive attitude and that night the compromised regiment burnt and plundered most of the sation, and then set out for Delhi. In the morning a feeble pursuit was ordered, after which the second native infantry regiment was disarmed. The mutineers, at Ferozepore thus taking advantage of this complacement attitude brokeout, plundered the magazines and took the road to Delhi,[3] but their attempts to reach Delhi were failed. They were promptly pursuid. brought back and blown from the guns. Those who escaped that tragic fate, perished in the rivers and jungles or were hunted down.[4]

JULLUNDUR

At Jullundur, the 6th Light Cavalry, the 36th and 61st Native Infantry and some Native Artillery were stationed. The 8th Foot and Horse with troops of Artillery were the European garrison Brigadier Hartley had been in command, but hed been succeeded by Brigadier M.C. Johnstone before the actual outbreak occussed

1. Mutiny Reports Vol. III, part II, p., 143.
2. The Panjab and Delhi in 1857 Vol. I, p. 104-109.
3. Mutiny Reports. Vol. VIII, Part II, pp. 331-345-46'
4. Mutiny Coresrpondence, Vol. II Part I, p. 26

at Jullundur.[1] The District was of importance, as one of the main lines of communication between the Panjab and Delhi passed through it, and was commanded, where it crossed the Satluj, by the Phillaur fort. Besides, being rich in agricultural resources, it was able to supply ample means of carriage and other necessaries of an army in the field. Two guns were equipped for service in any part of the District where required.

The tahsil at Jullundur City was strengthened to serve as a fort; the men of the Sher-Dil[2] regiment were called in from the district; the treasure was placed under an European guard, and all the Europeans were brought together. The Raja of Kapurthala,[3] Randhir Singh, was asked for help. He proceeded to Jullundur with all the troops he could collect, and with his brother remained there the whole of the hot weather. To his influence, the peace of the town and district was largely due.[4]

Unrest at Jullundur

There was a mutinous spirit in the native regiments. Constant fires had occured in the Cantonments and other signs of bad feeling had been manifested, but the military authorities disregarded these warning, placed confidence in their men, neglected the opportunity for disarming them, and when, the crisis came, were found unprepared. At 11 P.M. on June 7th, a fire broke out in Cantonments. When the officers went down to extinguish it, they were fired on and many of them wounded, some mortally. All the native troops, with the exception of the artillery, which opened on the mutineers with grape, and of some

1. The Civil Officers were the Commissioner, Major Lake, the Deputy Commissioner, Captain Farrington, the Assistant Commissioner, Mr S. S. Hogg. and the Extra Assistant Commissioner Mr. G. Knox.
2. Sher-Dil Regiment was first formed by Maharaja Ranjit Singh.
3. The Ahluwalia Sirdar had been given the title of Raja for good service rendered during the Second Sikh War.
4. He subsequently sent a detachment to Hoshirpur, and in all supplied 1,200 cavalry and 5 guns. In 1858, when the Jullundur Doab was no longer in danger, he, accompanied by his brother, Bikrama Singh marched with his troops to Oudh where they did excellent service.

fractions from each regiment, were in open mutiny, the cavalry the worst offenders and urging on the infantry whenever the latter seemed to waver. Some of the native soldiers showed much courage and devotion in saving the lives of their officers.

The object of the mutinous troops was now to get to Delhi: and as the City, Civil Station and Jail lay in the opposite direction and were, moreover, guarded by the Kapurthala troops, they escaped unharmed. The mutineers were supposed to have left Jullundur in two bodies about 1 A.M. on June 8th. One went off in an orderly manner towards Hoshiarpur and marching 130 miles in 54 hours, made good its escape along the hills. The second and larger party made for Phillaur, which they reached the same morning. Here they were joined by the 3rd Native Infantry, and got a boat with which some of them crossed the river and brought over more boats, and the whole party crossed during the day.[1]

PHILLAUR

The change of garrison at Phillaur the largest arsenal in the Panjab was better managed. In the absense of Brigadier Johnstone at Simla, the command of the Jullundur cantonment, twenty-four miles from Phillaur was held by Colonel Hartley of the 8th Queen's, who, hearing the news from Delhi put a company of his men into conveyances and wheeled them down to the Phillaur fort, whereupon Thomas Atkins marched in and Jack Sepoy walked out. A detachment of Europeans secretly marched off, and obtained possession of the fort, without having any suspicion. Arrangements were, immediately effected during that night for the telegraphic communications from inside the fort. A messenger was also despatched to Ludhiana to apprise Ricketts, the Deputy Commissioner to warn him to guard

1. Locally it is said that the crossing was effected at Kariana and Lisara, five and nine miles respectively up the river and this seems correct. On the south side of Satluj they were encountered by Mr. Ricketts, the Deputy Commissioner of Ludhiana with three companies of the 4th Sikhs under Lieut. Williams, two Nabha guns and some irregular match-lock men and troopers; but he was unable to prevent them advancing on Ludhiana and taking possession of the fort.

the bridge of boats across the Satluj with some of the 9th Irregular Cavalry, in case the mutineers attempted to seize or destro it.[1] Having thus fully fortified, reinforcement were sent from here to Delhi alongwith a strong detachments of troops, horse and foot, belonging to the Raja of Nabha, who had been requested to do so by Mr. Barnes, on the first news of the outbreak.[2]

LUDHIANA PLUNDERED

As at Meerut and Ferozepore, there was no pursuit but, on the river's left bank the mutineers, three thousand strong, encountered Rickets, the civilian Deputy Commissioner of Ludhiana.

Mr. Ricketts had a most difficult part to play, and ably did he acquit himself. The town of Ludhiana commanded the high road Delhi to the Panjab. It stood on the bank of the Satluj at the head af the bridge of boats connecting India with the Panjab proper. It was filled with a dissolute, lawless mixed population and other piratery races.

There was a fort at Ludhiana without Europeans to guard it, a city without regular troops to restrain it, a district traversed by roads in every direction, joining the seven commercial towns which formed the emporia of its trade, and situated on a river which for months in the year was a mere net work of fordable creeks which could only be guarded by a cordon of regular troops. Mr. Ricketts had for his Jail and treasury-guard a company of enemies in the shape of a detachment of the 3rd Native Infantry, and on the breaking out of the mutiny received another company of the same regiment. As there was no dependence to be placed upon these men, he summoned the feudal chiefs and the independent States to send him troops.

The chiefs of Nabha and Malerkotla sent in their men, to whom the safety of the station was entrusted. Detachments of these troops were like wise charged with the protection of the eight high roads which intersected the District, of the ferries, the

1. The Panjab and Delhi in 1857, Vol I-Browne. pp. 113-114
2. The Panjab and Delhi in 1857, Vol I-Browne, pp. 113-114

fords and the *ghats*. The undisciplined Nabha troops unfortunately failed Mr. Ricketts in his hour of need. They would not follow the Jullundur Mutineers.

A handful of Sikhs, who blazed away at the cowardly sepoys until, ammunition being exhausted, the little force withdrew into the protection of Ludhiana fort. The mutineers followed, and joined by the town rabble, Kashmiris Gujars, Afghans and other, plundered and burnt the station. They continued their march to Delhi. As soon as they had disappeared, Ricketts exacted heavy compensation from the turbulent townsmen and outside Gujars, tried and executed the ring-leaders. With a small body of police and liberal use of lash, he maintained order until, Delhi taken, the reign of law was re-established.[1]

THE PESHAWAR VALLEY

In the Peshawar valley, exclusive of the corps of Guides at Hoti Mardan and some military police, there were three batteries of field and one of horse artillery and about 11,000 regulars, horse and foot. Two-third were Hindustanis of the Bengal army. The neighbouring hill tribes were hostile to the British, but there was perfect peace inside the valley. Thus the elements of danger were considerable. Luckily the outbreak of Meerut came to be known to the Commissioner on the night of the 11th May, with the further strange addition on the following morning that "the European troops are defending barracks.[2]"

The two most suspected native infantry regiments, the 64th, and 55th, with the largest number of Brahmins in their ranks, were at once crippled for intrigue. The former being distributed in detachments amongst the outposts, for Hindustanis. The latter transferred to Hoti Mardan to take the place of the Guides, who unlike the British regulars, were "neither strapped down nor braced up nor button-strangled." They wore their own loose dusky shirts and wide Pyjamas etc.

1. Ludhiana District Gazetteer, pp, 25-29.
The Panjab and Delhi in 1857. Vo. I-Browne, pp. 260-264
2. Mutiny Reports Vol. III, Part I. p. 334
The Indian Mutiny in Perspecture-George Mac-Munn, p. 73

The Guides had crossed the Indus at Attock on their march to Delhi, and two most tainted native infantry regiments had been segregated amidst a fanatically hostile Muslim population before bazaar cantonment. Country-side knew for certain that Delhi was in the hands of the Meerut mutineers, and British rule thence to Calcutta in process of extinction. The discovery found none of the hitherto subject or restrained forces of the valley and neighbourhood 8000 Hindustani troops, city rabble, peasantry all armed, and the hill tribes prepared for action. The local authorities, Brigadier Cotton, Herbert Edwardes (Commissioner) and John Nicholson (Deputy Commissioner), acted promptly, and on May 21 disarmed four of the five Bengal regiments of regulars still in the Peshawar cantonment.

The work, which had to be done against the protestations, was carried out with even greater ease and precision than was had been the case eight days before at Mianmir. For not only the overawing force of British troops much larger, but a body of cut-throat Afridis from the Khaiber Pass stood ready to act. Next day a mixed force was despatched to Hoti Mardan to disarm the 55th Native Infantry there.[1]

As the British infantry approached, the sepoys became panic-struck and stamped, for the hills. They were pursued, and captured by the hundred, whilst the 500 who escaped into the mountains were hunted down by the Swatis and other tribesmen and killed to the last man. Their unfortunate Colonel, unable to bear the disgrace and destruction of the corps he had loved and trusted to the last, and convinced that his men had been terrorised into flight, committed suicide. The facile disarming of four regiments, annihilation of the fifth, and segregation of another for the time the native cavalry, all irregulars, and some of the infantry were allowed to retain their arms and treated as loyalists-convinced the people that the English were .masters still, and going to win at Delhi. Edwardes was quick to take advantage of that trend of public opinion by offering service to every able-bodied dare-devil in and outside the valley. It was a move which conducted more

1. Mutiny Reports, Vol. VIII. Part II, p. 136.

to the peace and contentment of the country than the presence of an additional brigade.[1]

AMBALA

It was known for some weeks previous to the outbreak that minds of the Indian soldiers in this station were unsettled. On the 19th April mysterious fires began to occur, and though they were at first attributed to the thatchers, the eyes of all the residents were gradually opened to see that the soldiery and none others were the real authors of those fires. Mr. Forsyth obtained positive information, on the 7th and 8th May, that the prediction of rebellious clique among the sepoys was "that in the following week blood would be shed at Delhi or Ambala, and that a general rising of the sepoys would take place,"[2] On May 10th, the day of the Meerut mutiny, the 5th and 60th Regiments, Indian infantry, and the detache d guard of the 60th at the treasury, simultaneously rushed to their bells of arms, and began loading their muskets. The treasury guard remained under arms the whole day in direct disobedience to orders.

As soon as this first difficulty had been overcome, the necessity for preserving the peace of the District led Mr. Barnes to call on the commutation-tenure chiefs to furnish men instead of their usual tribute in money. By the operation of this order a force of 459 foot and 259 horse was soon at his disposal, but the moral effect of those and the other influential chiefs siding with the British was of far greater value than even the force they supplied.[3] Mr. Barnes observes further :—

"In addition to these Jagirdars, who were bound to supply levies, several public-spirited individuals volunteered their own services and brought several followers. Among these the most prominent were Rao, Rahim Bakhsh, of Panjlasa, who with 50 followers guarded the road between Ambala and Jagadhri and the Sirkardars of Sadhaura, who furnished 60 men to protect

1. Mutiny Reports, Vol. VIII. Part II, p. 136.
Mutiny Correspondence Vol. VII, Part I p. 64.
The Panjab and Delhi in 1857, Vol I, pp. 138, 140, 151.
2. The Mutiny Reports, Vol. VIII, Part II, p. 140.
3, The Panjab and Delhi in 1857, Vol I-Browne, pp. 42-48.

the public and private buildings in the civil station, thus relieving our police from very heavy duty."[1]

MULTAN

In contrast with the flasco at Jullundur was the success of the procedure carried out at Multan. As the only British troops in the station were 48 artillery men in the fort, whilst outside there were two native infantry regiments. John Lawrence had long considered that the attempt at disarming value should be deferred until some of the troops on their way up from Sindh should reach Multan and that, when made, the Bengal infantry alone should be disarmed. However, when the outbreak at Jullundur had occurred, he wired to Multan advising immediate action before the news should circulate in the sepoy lines.

At the time of the outbreak it was occupied by the 62nd and 69th Native Infantry, Ist Irregular Cavalry a native troop of horse artillery, and a company of European Artillery men. The 69th was strongly suspected. The other native troops were considered staunch, and subsequent events verified the supposition in every case. It was necessary to provide a refuge in case of any disturbance. The old fort, which had lain in a ruinous condition since it had been battered and dismantled by the British army in 1849, was put in a position of defence, provisioned, and garrisoned by some men of Captain Tronson's Kuttar Mukhi police battalion. As these arrangements occupied some days, and the temper of the native troops could not be trusted from hour to hour Lieutenant Etheridge of the Indian Navy, who happened to be at Multan with his vessel, was requested to detain the steamer until the fort should have become defensible.[2]

Colonel Hicks, commanding at Multan, failed to discover in the conduct of the regiments of native infantry anything which could justify him in taking from them their arms. The Chief Commissioner, however, sent preemptory orders that they were to be disarmed, and on the morning of June 10th the minds of European and native residents were relieved, commerce was re-established, and the British authority vindicated by the most successful disarming of the 62nd and 69th Native Infantry by Major C. Chamberlain, commanding 1st

1. The Mutiny Reports, Vol. VIII, Part I, p. 230.
2. The Panjab and Delhi in 1857, Vol. I-Browne, pp. 127-128.

Irregular Cavalry. The peculiar character of this excellent move was that the European troops were but 48 artillery men. The other auxiliaries were all native and one regiment, the 1st Irregular Cavalry, was composed of Hindustanis.[1]

On the 11th August the horse atillerry was disarmed as a precautionary measure. On the same date the enrolment of men for the new 11th Panjab Infantry was commenced by transferring to it men from other regiments. The Gugera insurrection broke out little more than a month afterwards. The new men at Multan were still undisciplined, and could hardly yet be relied on as a serviceable field force. Most of them were left to guard the station, while Major Chamberlain led out his regiment, the Ist Irregular Cavelry (Hindustanis), with some 200 men of the new levies, against the insurgents.[2]

Another cause of anxiety at Multan had been the conduct of the preventive service on the Satluj. Most of the men employed in it were Hindustanis. They bolted at the first rise in India and went off in numbers to join their kindred by blood and by disposition who were enjoying a transient glory over the smouldering ruins of Hansi and Hissar. Men to take their place were raised in the district, and no serious damage was done to the Government interest by their defection. Under the orders of the Chief Commissioner a camel train was organized, having one of its Depots at Multan. It was designed for the conveyance of private parcels, munitions of war and merchandise between Sind and the Panjab. It proved most useful.[3]

MUTINY AT MULTAN

The 62nd and 69th Native Infantry Regiments, though disarmed, were kept in cantonment for some months, until in June 1858 orders were issued for their disbandment. In order to prevent the assembly of large bodies of disaffected persons at one spot, it was decided that the disbandment should be carried out gradually in daily bands of 20 men. This order gave rise to the belief that it was the intention of Government either to massacre them in small bodies or to arrange for their seizure

1. The Mutiny Reports, Vol. VIII Part I, p. 253.
2. The Panjab and Delhi in 1857, Vol. II-Browne, pp. 204-205.
3. The Panjab and Delhi in 1857, Vol. I-Browne, p. 269.

on the way to their homes in Hindustan and for their subsequent transportation. The feelings of alarm thus engendered were fostered by mischief-makers and towards the end of August 1858, rumours were current that the disbanded regiments intended to mutiny. No adequate measures were taken to allay their fears and the precautions against the outbreak appear to have been insufficient. On August 31st practically the whole of both regiments mutined while on parade; they made attacks on the European Artillery and their old lines; murdered the artillerymen; and then broke away in various directions.[1]

Of about twelve hundred who mutined, some three hundred were killed in cantonments, while the remainder escaped into the district. One party numbering about 400, fled southwards past Sher Shah and Shujabad, pursued closely by the tahsildar of the latter place, the followers of the Makkdam of Sher Shah and the local yeomanry and peasants. At night they split up into two parties, the smaller of which was driven into a low marshy island in the Chenab, while the larger followed the river towards its junction with the Satluj. The members of the former body were either drowned in the river or killed or captured by the police and local leaders. The second party was overtaken a few days later by Lieutenant Norgate, who had been sent from Multan with a detachment of cavalry and infantry, and although the mutineers fought desperately, they were practically annihilated.

Another body of rebels had fled northwards up the Chenab, where they were pursued by a detachment of cavalry which, however, failed to intercept them and the mutineers, crossing the Lahore Road, turned southwards and fled through the bar in the direction of Luddan on the Satluj. An immediate attack was made and the rebels were completely defeated. No quarter was given and no prisoners were taken. The other mutineers who had escaped from Multan were captured one by one and within a few days of the rising all were accounted for.[2]

Advance On Delhi

The advance was begun from Ambala on May 25, but a

1. The Panjab and Delhi in 1857, Vol. I-Browne, pp. 266-268.
2. The Mutiny Reports, Vol VIII, Part II. pp. 255-260.
   The Panjab and Delhi in 1857, Vol. I-Browne, pp, 266-68.

day or two afterwards, General Anson died of cholera at Karnal. Sir Henry Barnard then at Ambala, succeeded him. Though new to India and wanting experience, he was energetic, and pushed on. joined by a weak brigade from Meerut, he brushed aside a fainthearted attempt by the mutineers to bar his progress, and by June 9, reinforced by the invaluable Guides from Hoti Mardan, who had covered 580 miles in twenty-two days, planted himself and his four thousand men, with 20 field-guns. A few pieces of heavy ordinance were received from Phillaur, on the historic "ridge" in Delhi about a mile from the north-west corner of the city, and directly facing its Kashmiri and Morigates were with him [1]

The arrival of the Moveable Column in August put a new life in the war-worn besiegers on the Ridge and enabled General Winson to launch the final attack. The last reinforcements (including a siege train) arrived from the Panjab on september 6 ; eight days later the Kashmiri Gate was blown. The city had fort fell after six days of desperate resistance by the mutineers who contested every inch of space. The fall of Delhi rang the death knell of the Mutiny[2], as the rebels had concentrated most of their strength there. They never regained their confidence again and their subsequent moves lacked the pristine vigour and enthusiasm. Bahadur Shah, though the nominal head of the movement, was a symbol round which all anti-British elements had gathered. His exile led to the disruption of the rebel force. The insurgents missed the one to whom their loyalty and honour bound them. With his exit from the scene, the crucial phase of the Revolt was over. After the fall of Delhi the Rebellion entered a stage which was as disorganised as it was luckless. After September, the British fought with ease and confidence. Their victory was never in doubt.

Having got the nucleus of an Anglo-Panjab army before Delhi, John Lawrence's next business was to maintain it there-to feed it with men, munitions, and supplies-until such time as it should be in position to strike effectually. For the present

1. The Panjab and Delhi in 1857, Vol. II-Browne pp. 173-179. The Mutiny Correspondence, Vol. VII, Part II, p. 391.
2. The Tale of the Great Mutiny-Fitcheat, p. 270.

therefore, the fighting manhood of the province responded in thousands to John Lawrence's call to arms ; but he chose his recruits wisely, so balancing antagonistic nationalities and creeds as to give dangerous preponderance to none. Between the middle of May and end of August he enlisted in all thirty-four thousand men, almost the exact equivalent to Hindustanis sooner or latter disarmed.

The recovery of Delhi having been mainly due to the unremitting exertions of John Lawrence and his brilliant subordinates, the Governor-General deemed it fitting that the Imperial City with the surrounding territory should be placed under Government of the man who had reclaimed it from the grasp of the rebels. Accordingly on February, 1858, the Delhi Territory lying on the right of the Jamna, together with the territory confiscated from the rebel Nawabs of Jhajjar and Bahadurgarh, was transferred from the North-Western provinces to the Panjab. Though politically a part of the Panjab, this area, which corresponds to the present Ambala division, is, in language, religion, and racial characteristics, more nearly allied to Hindustan. At the commencement of 1859 the enlarged Province was placed under a separate Lieutenant-Governor. Sir John Lawrence was the first to hold office.

The Hindustani regiments that were disbanded were sent to their homes ; and four regiments of Panjab cavalry and seventeen of infantry, raised during the Mutiny, were transferred to the Bengal army to supply their place. Rewards in the shape of grants of territory were made to the Sikh Chiefs of Patiala, Jind and Nabha for the services rendered during the Mutiny ; and a large estate of Oudh was conferred upon the Raja of Kapurthala.

Minor Disturbances

Throughout the period of the Mutiny with the exception of the Gogera (in Montgomery district) rising, no mass up risings took place in the Panjab. The Hindustan troops broke out at several places[1]

1. The following mutinous outbreaks of sepoys took place in the Panjab:-
   (a) Ferozepore, May 14th the large portion of the 45th and 57th Native Infantry broke out.
   (b) Hoti Mardan 21st-55th Native Infantry. *(Contd. on Page 90)*

and endeavoured to gain popular support but in vain. The people of the Panjab extended no friendly hand to them. The mutineers, therefore found themselves like unwelcomed guests in a strange land. The mutinous outbreak did not occur simultaneously. They were isolated risings and took their place at different places, at different times. Due to the policy of disarmament, carried out by John Lawrence's assistants with striking suddenness, the mutineers lost the initiative which they were never able to regain afterwards. Forestalled in many places by the action of the authorities, the disaffected regiments had no other alternative but to bide their time till they could find opportunity to join their comrades at Delhi.

Here and there, some of the Muslim tribes-under British rule had begun to lose status and means of easy subsistence. They were growing restive as the weeks lengthened and rumours of British disasters were circulated. The first to break out against order were the Gujars, from the Kaghan glen in Hazara. About Ludhiana and southwards bands of them collected, and began plundering, but having neither cohesion, and intelligence nor firearms, were easily suppressed.

From time to time other tribes in the same neighbourhood, such as Ranghars and the gipsy fraternities, known as "the criminal tribes," also attempted risings, but were at once hunted down by police and levies, and terrorised into their normal condition of offensive uselessness. Later, the Kharrals and Dhunds of the hills between Hazara and Rawalpindi had made a combined movement against the hill sanitorium, murree, but their insurrection fizzled out at the sight of a few policemen. Then, towards the end of the long tension in the third month of the struggle before Delhi, an insurrection on a large scale

---

(Contd. from Page 89)

(c) Jullundur, June 7th-6th Light Cavalry, 36th and 61st Native Infantry.
(d) Phillur, June 8th-3rd Native Infantry.
(e) Jhelum, July 7th-Part of the 14th Light Cavalry.
(f) Sialkot, July 9th-A wing of the 8th Light Cavalry and 46th Native Infantry.
(g) Thanesar, July 14th-Part of the 5th Native Infantry.
(h) Lahore, July 30th-26th Native Infantry.
(i) Ferozepore, August 19th-10th Light Infantry,
(j) Peshawar, August 29th-51st Native Infantry,
(k) Ambala, September 30th-remnants of 5th and 60th Native Infantry.
(l) Mianwali, in the Leiah District-30 men of 9th Irregular Cavalry.

broke out amongst the pastoral Muslim tribes, inhabiting the jungly tracts betweeen Lahore and Multan. Though their largest gang under their leader Ahmad Khan, took, sacked, and for some days occupied a small town, Kot Kamalia, their rebellion was never formidable.

Effects on the Panjab

There were positive and far reaching effects of the fall of Delhi on the course of the Mutiny in India, but its effects on the Panjab were still more decisive. The first week of September had seen the wave of excitement sweeping from the Indus to the Satluj. In the second week, risings actually broke out and threatened to envelope the whole province. Had the Mughal capital not fallen by the end of September, the land of the Five Rivers too, would have come into the vortex of rebellion.[1] The news of the victory was well received throughout the province. The wavering and the ill-disposed hastened to offer congratulations to the authorities and seized the opportunity of re-establishing their reputation for loyalty. Everywhere the people showed their eagerness to be recruited in the punitive expeditions, "The stubborn and gallant resistance of the Rani of Jhansi and other stirring events of the final phase of the Great Revolt left the Panjab perfectly unruffled."[2]

Achievements of John Lawrence

Before the Mutiny burst forth, John Lawrence had only shown himself as an efficient provincial administrator and as such he was recognised in India. Six months later the whole English speaking world hailed him as a great statesman, who by his energy, resolution and farsightedness had saved the British Empire in India. "One man (John Lawrence), however, must never be forgotten while Englishmen remember Delhi......the saviour of India.[3]" The period of crisis did not bring forth any new characteristics but rather saw the grand culmination of the qualities, he had hitherto displayed on a smaller scale. As early as 1848, when the flames of the Multan-Rebellion were fast spreading into the districts, Lawrence had acted with the same promptitude and decision. In fact his efficient administration of the

1. The Mutiny Reports, Vol. VIII, Part II, p. 369.
2. The Mutiny Reports, Vol. VIII, Part I, p. 205.
3. Lord Lawrence, Vol. I-Trotter, p. 229.

Jullundur Doab had revealed him as a man who could be relied on to face a still greater crisis with greater equanimity. An all India crisis like the Mutiny provided an opportunity for the full flowering of his personality. We have seen how like a statesman he surveyed the emergency and then calmly set to grapple with it.

The vigour and thoroughness with which John Lawrence tackled multifarious problems, were also very striking. He had a dual task at hand. One was to maintain a firm grip over the province and the other was to organise the transport and reinforcements for Delhi. But he rose equal to the occasion. His energy, as Temple has put it, was "resplendent, as it was all pervading, life infusing and ranging in all directions with the broadest sweep." Edward Thornton wrote of him, "Looking back now on all that happened, I can see clearly that it was he and none of his subordinates who can be said to have saved the Punjab.[1]" Herbert Edwardes with his characteristic candour declared "Any treatment of the picture that would put John in other than the first place would be thoroughly untrue.[2]"

The role played by John Lawrence in the stirring drama of 1857, constitutes the most brilliant chapter of his life-the chapter which reveals to us all the different facts of his character. Never perhaps had any administrator of the East India Company shown such a perfect union of organisation, energy and foresight. Mr. Fitcheat rightly wrote "he could survey the situation with the balanced judgment of an Englishman ; could choose his course with the shrewd and calculating sagacity of a Scotchman ; then carry it out with Irish fire and daring.[3]" Such were the achievements of the man who on February, 1859 broken down in health, relinquished his charge and sailed for England. Little did he knew at that time that he was to return five years later as Viceroy and Governor-General of India.

From the first January, 1859 A.D., the Panjab and its dependencies were constituted under Lieutenant-Governorship. Sir John Lowrence, who had hitherto held the office of Chief Commissioner, was appointed the first Lieutenant Gavernor, with his Headquarters at Lahore. He was, however, compelled by ill health to vacate his office at the end of February, and to leave for England.

1. Quoted by Aitcheson-Lord Lawrence, p. 111.
2. Quoted by Aitcheson-Lord Lawrence, p. 111.
3. The tail of the Great Mutiny-Fitcheat, p. 267.

4

Panjab During 1859-1871

(Sir Robert Montgomery 1859-1865)

Early life

Sir Robert Montgomery (1808-1887) was born in 1808. He was the son of Samuel Law Montgomery, rector of Lower Moville, Donegal. He was educated at Foyle College, London-derry and at Warxall Hall School (North Willtshire). He was appointed to the Bengal Civil Service in 1827 A. D. He filled various subordinate posts, as that of a Magistrate and collector of Allahadad, on the recommendation of Sir Henry Montgomery Lawrence, his old friend and school fellow. Then he was transferred by Lord Dalhousie to the Panjab where he took a large part in organising the newly annexed province. He occupid successfully arduous and responsible posts of Commissioner of the Lahore division in 1849. After this he was appointed the member of the Panjab Board of Administration on which he succeeded Charles Grenville Mansel in 1850. Eventually on the dissolution of the Board of Administration in 1853, he was appointed Judicial Commissioner.

Member of the Board

The duties of Robert Montgomery were not merely legal, but also included the superintendence of education, road, police and municipalities. It was in the early days of the Mutiny of 1857, that he had to perform his greatest and most signal service. He disarmed the sepoys at Lahore on 13 May, 1857, when the telegraph brought to Lahore the news of the capture of Delhi by the mutineers on May 12, 1857 John Lawrence the Chief Commissioner was then at Rawalpindi, beyond reach of telegrams. Montgomery was the Chief Civil Officer in

Lahore. No sooner did he get the news that the four native regiments cantoned at Mian Mir, were ready to rise as soon as they heard that the Delhi troops, had revolted against the British rule, then he summoned his chief civil officers, he ordered to disarm the troops immediately.[1]

Simultaneously Montgomery caused three British companies to disarm the sepoys in the Lahore fort. He despatched a company of the 81st later in the day, to make Amritsar and the fortress of Gobindgarh safe. He further timely alerted Ferozepur, Multan and Kangra, and called on his local officials to place their treasure incharge of the nearest British troops, and to be on their guard. This wise temerity of Montgomery was of inestimable service to the English cause in India at that critial juncture.[1]

Lieutenant Governor

On the 26th February, 1859, he was appointed Lieutenant Governor of the Panjab, and held that post till 1865, when he resigned and returned to England on pension. In 1869, he was a appointed member of the Council of Secretary of State for India. This office he held until his death on 28th December, 1887 in London.

The Penal Code 1862

It was during his time that the Penal Code was extended to the Panjab in 1862. The Sessions cases were fewer than in former years. It was owing to the District Magistrates who disposed of all cases in which 7 years' imprisonment was considered sufficient punishment.

The Judicial Commissioner commented upon the very large number of cases (1,174) disposed of by the District Magistrates, in the exercise of the inhanced powers conferred upon them under the Act XV of 1862, and the comparatively small number (262) cases disposed of by Sessions Judges. "Not only", observed the Judicial Commissioner "did these cases add materially to the work of Deputy Commissioners, who were in general, fully occupied with their own proper duties. and little able to bear the extra burden thrown upon them; but the cases being disposed of by the District officers, were not always treated with the same care and deliberation and judgment

1. The Dictionary of National Biography, Vol, XIII, pp. 770-771.

which they could obtain in the Court of Sessions, while the accused were also deprived of the right of appeal to the highest court."[1]

Powers of The Financial Commissioners

Act XXVII of 1865, empowered the local government to invest the Financial Commissioner for the purpose of hearing appeals in respect of suits regarding land, or the rent, revenue or produce of land, until the establishment of a Chief Court, with two or more judges[2].

This act was passed with a view of relieving the Judicial Commissioner, who was unable to dispose, single-handed of the large increase of work resulting from the transfer of appeals regarding land, or the rent, revenue or produce of land, to the Judicial Department, under, the provisions of Act XIX of 1865. The office of the Judicial Commissioner was abolished, and a Chief Court, consisting of two judges, was created in Lahore with final appellate authority in civil and criminal cases. The first civilian judge was Mr. H.A. Roberts, who had been Judicial Commissioner and a Barrister-Judge was Mr. Charles Boulnois.

Constitution of The Court of Judicature

Act IV of 1866, was a re-enactment of the provisions of Act XXVII of 1865, to the legality of which objection had been raised owing to a technical informality in the passing thereof. This act was generally known as an Act to amend the constitution of the Chief Court of Judicature in the Panjab and its dependencies. In addition to the above acts, Acts of the Legislature were extended to the Panjab such as the pleader's, Mukhtiar's and Revenue Agent's Act.[3]

At the close of the year 1869, there were exclusive of Settlement courts, 540 tribunals of various kinds for disposal of criminal Civil or Revenue cases, or one tribunal to every 32, 400 personnel. These tribunals included :–

1. Panjab Administration Report-1863-64, paras 24 & 26.
2. Panjab Administration Report-1867-68, paras 64 &65.
3. Panjab Administration Report-1866-67, para 65.

(1) The Chief Court, consisting of three Judges (one of them a Barrister), the final appellate authority in Civil and Criminal cases, and exercising the powers of a Court of original jurisdiction in cases, where European British subjects were charged with serious offences.

(2) The Court of the Financial Commissioner, exercising final appellate jurisdiction in Civil suits regarding land in districts where a settlement was in progress.

(3) Twelve Divisional Courts of Sessions and Appeal.

(4) Thirty-two Courts of District Officers.

(5) One hundred and nineteen Courts of Assistants to District Officers, Native and European.

(6) Eight District Small Cause Courts.

(7) Esght Cantonment Courts.

(8) Seven Boards of Honorary Magistrates in towns.

(9) Two hundred and six Courts of Tehsildars and Naib-Tehsildars.

(10) Twenty-two District Honorary Magistrates, known as "Jagirdar Magistrates."[1]

Settlements Effected

Mr. Princep became Settlement Commissioner in 1863. He had the immediate direction of the revised Settlements of Amritsar, Gurdaspur and Sialkot, with Assistants working under him and the control of the revised Settlements of Lahore, Gujranwala, Gujrat and Montgomery: to which separate Settlement Officers were appointed. During this period in revision of the records of rights

1. The remainder includes of the Courts of Canal, Forest, and Customs Officers and Officers in charge of Jails, who were vested with Magisterial powers for limited and specific purposes.
Of the Judges, one was a Barrister, 49 were Covenanted Civil Servants (of whom two were Barrister), 91 were Military Officers (of whom one was a Barrister), 89 were Uncovenanted English Civil Servants, and 385 were Natives.

in Kangra was effected by Mr. J.B. Lyall, and the first regular settlement of Hazara and Peshawar were begun by Captain Wace and Captain Hastings.

Lenient Policy of Assessment

The Panjab government was strongly in favour of very lenient assessment. The province at that time was on the eve of a great development of trade and an extraordinary rise in the money value of agricultural produce, but it was doubted whether any very large increase of revenue was likely to be secured in future. The main object of the British government was to keep the country quiet and content and to encourage agricultural improvements. The policy of making settlements permanent in well-developed tracts was under discussion, and had been accepted in principle by the orders issued by the Secretary of State, in 1862 A.D.

FAMINES-1860-1900

Early History

The first famine in the Panjab, according to the earlier sources available occurred in 1783-84 A.D. It was popularly called the '*CHALISA, KAL*[1]. It effected the whole country from the Satluj to Allahabad, and was acute in the neighbourhood of Delhi. Hariana was desolated and the people perished in great number while many had immigrated to far distant places. 'The shopkeeper hid in his house and the child wept over its meals,' was a popular saying of a famine fifty years later. 'Two only,' it was said. 'have survived, the traders and the butcher, the one by using his scales, the other by using his knife.' Never is the butcher busier than when the rain falls, as anyone knows who has seen villages after villages strewn with the bones and carcases of starving cattle slaughtered for their hides. At such a time fodder was so scarce, that any bit of scrap that cattle would eat was guarded as jealously as if it were a valuable crop of sugarcane. Every tree, too, is looped to the bark and there was no more desolating sight than the long roadside avenues raising flayed, twisted arms

1. The Famine of the year forty.

to a bare pitiless sky. After a bad famine there were villages where not a cow, buffalo or calf was to be seen. In 1869, 300,000 cattle perished in the single district of Hissar, and a few years later Rohtak lost 37 per cent of its stock. 'An ox,' it was said, 'sold for a piece of bread, and a camel for farthing. The carts, too were idle for the oxen were dead, and the bride went to the bridegroom's house with rites half done."[1]

Few villages in the area, spoke about the heavy loss of lives due to that famine. In 1833-34, the conditions were those of severe scarcity rather than of famine ; and though there was suffering in Hissar and Rohtak Districts and the Fazilka tahsil, no relief, beyond large suspensions of revenue, was given. The scarcity was, however, the precursor of serious famine in 1837-38, when the tract between Allahabad and Delhi was most seriously affected. Relief works were opened for the able-bodied, but the relief of the infirm and helpless was left to private charity. The main features of this famine were the prevalence of aimless wandering and the extraordinary amount of violent crime.

A Peep Through the Causes

The cultivator had no rights to trade with, and little concern beyond raising and harvesting his crops. All beyond this was managed for him by the State farmer or revenue officer or the village headman ; and the village in subservience to the local authorities." The general rule of life was that the harvest suffised for the current needs. The immediate requirements for human life—food and warmth—were easily satisfied by soil and climate. There was little or no spur to increased effort, little need to look ahead; little scope for enterprise and little reward for labour in excess of the customary. Under such conditions, progress as then measured, of necessity lagged : the accumula-tion of wealth was slow, and it was not easy to see that internal forces there were which would, unaided, had broken the circle.

Bumper harvests merely caused a glut; they served to replenish the stores but went little further towards strengthening the community

1. The Panjab Peasant in Prosperity & Debt-Darling-p, 92

against the strain of calamity. A severe drought on the other hand caused immense economic loss. The former could not counterbalance the latter. The trading community of the time could not find markets to absorb the surplus of the one or to meet deficiency of the other; its own development was the result of contemporary normal requirements, and neither the pressing demands of a year of famine nor the surplus of a bounteous harvest was sufficient to bring into being the higher organisation of commerce and communications without which its special needs could not be met.

There was needed a steadily recurring movement of commodities, a normal surplus over local consumption in one area and a normal demand for this surplus in another. Recurrent famines were not of themselves sufficient to bring about the production of a surplus or to sustain the machinery to dispose of that surplus or even to bring in to being the means for their own remedy. They occurred at too long intervals in any one area to stimulate a developmnt of trade and communications in that area sufficient to cope with such a crisis. For trade in food-grains and other goods, steady volume for sale is essential.

The market required steady feeding, neither gorging in a season of plenty nor starving in one of drought. The position was thus practically stabilised: no organization for trade and commerce could grow up without the production of goods surplus to the local demand, and no individual, no village and no province could continue to produce such a surplus unless there were in existence the machinery of trade and commerce to ensure for it a reward commensurate with the labour expended.[1]

Famine 1860-69

The famine of 1860-61 affected only the Districts between the Jamuna and the Satluj, and was the result partly of the Mutiny, and partly of the deficient rainfall in the two preceding years, followed by a failure of the Monsoon in 1860. The principles adopted in 1833-34 were again followed. Gratuitous relief was given mainly in the form of cooked food.

Practically the same tract was again affected in 1868-69, but the great influx of famine-stricken immigrants from Rajasthan exhausted

---

1. The Wealth and Welfare of the Panjab-H. Calvert, pp. 10-11

the resources of private charity. The principle that it was the duty of the people to relieve the infirm and weak had to be abanboned, and Government acknowledged its liability to supplement charitable aid. Large works under professional control and minor works under civil officers were also utilized for affording relief. The excess mortality in the two Provinces was estimated at 1, 200,000. About 3 lakhs of revenue was remitted in the Panjab.[1]

Amritsar Affected

During the years 1868-69, the city of Amritsar increased the difficulties for its reputed wealth made it the centre to which distressed persons were attracted both from British and other territory, and there were at one time frequented by thousand people in the city and its neighbourhood, subsisting wholly upon charity.

Relief works were started on which labour was paid for at famine rates, such as roads from Taran Tarn to Jandiala, Vairowal, and Hari-ke-ghat, and from the city of Amritsar to Ajnala. Houses from which the poor might be fed were started in Amritsar city and at the tahsils head-quarters. The work of filling in the great ditch from which the materials for the ramparts had been excavated, and which was a fruitful source of disease, were begun. Nearly three thousand labourers a day were employed on this work alone. The works were brought to a close in April, 1869, after the rain had removed the main fear of famine, but had to be re-opened in August, when the usual rains again failed. This time the Ahluwalia Dhab, a morass in the centre of the city, was taken up and from first to last nearly a lakh of labourers were employed on filling it up.[2]

The Great Famine 1877-97

The great famine of 1877-78 hardly reached this Province, in which only scarcity existed. Fazilka and the Districts of the Delhi division, which were not protected by irrigation, suffered most. But after 1878, in spite of occasional short harvests, the Panjab had a respite from actual scarcity till 1896-97. In 1895 the Monsoon ceased early in August, and a poor Autumn harvest was

1. Panjab Administration Report, 1869-70, p. 1
2. The Panjab Peasant i.. Prosperity & Debt-Darling, pp. 92-99

followed by a deficient spring crop in 1896. In the later year failure of the Monsoon caused widespread scarcity as in other parts of India. The whole of the Delhi Division, except Simla, and parts of the Lahore and Rawalpindi Divisions were affected. A total of two and half million day-units were relieved of whom half were in Hissar. Relief cost twenty two lakhs, Two hundred twenty one lakhs of land revenue was suspended, and at the close of the famine eleven and half lakhs was advanced for the purchase of seed and cattle.

After a prosperous year the Monsoon failed again in 1898 and 1899, and it supervened in the same tracts. The scarcity of fodder caused immense mortality among cattles and the distress among the people was intense. Relief was afforded to fifty two million day-units at a cost of 48 lakhs. In addition, 44 lakhs of land revenue was suspended and 19 lakhs granted for the purchase of seed and cattle as soon as favourable rain fell in the autumn of 1900. The Charitable Relief Fund also allotted 12 lakhs to the Panjab. Hissar was again the most deeply affected tract, accounting for two thirds of the numbers relieved.

Effects On Population

The immediate effects of scarcity on the population of the Province had been practically negligible. The famine of 1899-1900, the most severe since annexation of the Panjab, affected the health of the people, so that many were unable to withstand disease which under more favourable circumstances might not have proved fatal. It might have been anticipated that the two famines of the decade 1891-1900 would have appreciably affected the population in Hissar and Rohtak Districts, but the Census of 1901 showed an increase of 5,711 since 1891 in the former, and an increase of nearly 10 percent in the latter. Generally speaking, as regards mortality, the after effects of famine were almost more potent than famine itself.

Practically no deaths from actual starvation were recorded in the province in the famines. The cholera was most to be feared ; but when famine ceased, after a plentiful Monsoon, malaria, acting on a people whose vitality had been reduced by privation, claimed a long tale of victims. At such seasons the mortality was naturally greatest among the very old and the very young This is showed by the fact that, at the Census, Hissar returned only 999 children under five in every 10,000 of its population, as compared with the Provincial ratio of 1,340. This paucity of children, however, was to some extent due to a diminished birth-rate. The famine of 1899-1900 lasted exactly thirteen months from September, 1899. Upto December the birth-rate was fairly normal, but after that month it rapidly declined until the close of the famine.

In July, 1900, it was only 22.3 per mile, as compared with 40.5, the annual average for the month in the five years 1891-95. On the other hand, the re-establishment of normal conditions, after famine, was followed by an abnormally high birth-rate. Thus, in Hissar, famine ended in August, 1897. Upto July, 1898, the birth-rate remained low; but it then rose rapidly and remaind well above the average until September, 1899, the highest figures occurring in October and November, 1898, when they reached 81.7 and 76.7 per mile, as compared with 57 and 50.8 respectively, the averages for those two months in 1891-95.

Protective Measures By The Government

The British Government was ever eager to find out a permanent remedy against this menace. The means and remedies were actively considered by the Government. The two great remedies were the extension of railways and irrigation. As to the former, from the point of view of famine protection, the province was as a whole well off, and further schemes were in hand for facilitating distribution of the immense surplus stocks produced in the large canal colonies. As to the latter, much was done and much more was in contemplation. The Chenab and Jhelum Canals, by rendering cultivable vast areas of waste had been of incalculable help in reducing the pressure on the soil in the most thickly populated Districts, and in increasing the productive power of the province, but, until the insecure tracts themselves were rendered safe by the extension to them or irrigation, scarcity and famine could still be apprehended.[1]

1. The Panjab Peasant in Prosperity and Debt-Darling, pp. 91-92-98

THE AMBELA CAMPAIGN 1863-68

Sayyid Ahmad Shah of Bareilly

A mountain pass in Buner, is situated just beyond the northeast border of Peshawar District. The pass gave its name to the Ambela campaign of 1863. In !824, one Sayyid Ahmad Shah, the Pindari, settled with about forty followers among the Yusufzai tribes on the Peshawar border. This event occurred just after Ranjit Singh had gained his victory over the Pathans at Naushahra. Driven out of the Peshawar valley by the Sikhs in 1827, Sayyid Ahmad Shah sought refuge in Swat, and eventually in Buner, but in 1820 he seized Peshawar. His Pathan disciples, however, soon tired of his attempted reforms, drove him across the Indus to Balkot in Hazara. There he was attacked by the Sikhs under Maharaja Sher Singh and was defeated and slain.

Sayyid Akbar Shah

His surviving disciple sought a refuge at Sittana, a village of the Utamanzai Yusufzai. Here under Sayyid Akbar Shah, spiritual chief of Swat, the Hindustanis built a fort and established a colony, which soon became an asylum for political refugees, escaped criminals, and deserters from British India. After the annexation of the Panjab, this colony became a source of anxiety to the British Government, and in 1853 an invasion of the territory of the Khan of Ambela British feudatory, necessitated a punitive expedition. The fanatics displayed renewed activity in 1857, and in 1858 made daring attack on the camp of the British Assistant Commissioner of Mardan, necessitating a second punitive expedition. The tribes then agreed not to allow the colony to reoccupy Sittana, and they settled at Malka on the northern side of the Mahaban mountain.

From this settlement they renewed their depredations, which consisted chiefly in kidnapping Hindu traders from Hazara, and in 1863 they reoccupied Sittana. Drastic measures then became unavoidable, and two columns, one from Peshawar and the other from Hazara, were organised. The former under Sir Neville Chamberlain, 9,000 strong occupied the Ambela Pass, the object being to march through the Chamla valley and attack Sittana. The tribes of Buner and Swat, however, rose en masse and made repeated attacks on the

British positions in the pass. After protracted operations the pass was secured and the advance into the Chamla valley carried out ; but the expedition lost 20 officers.[1] The object of the expedition was, however, attained. Malka, which had been made the chief stronghold of the Hindustani fanatics, was destroyed by the people of Buner themselves as a guarantee of their submission.

For the Peshawar valley the conditions were different ; its large garrison being directly under the orders of the Commander in-Chief, and the Amir of Afghanistan and Viceroy corresponding with each other without the intervention of the provincial ruler. The Government of India necessarily closely supervised Peshawar frontier affairs, and, owing to local ignorance, sometimes burnt its fingers badly-e.g., in the Ambela war of 1863. The British misfortunes in that campaign, though immediately conducing to the appointment of John Lawrence as Viceroy, contributed later to supply forward politicians, with arguments for replacing his close-border system by one of aggressive activity. "Had we not, they contended, shut ourselves up behind a Chinese wall of forts and pillars, we should have known something of the country and its inhabitants between the British and their objective, Ambela, and their force would not have been hemmed in and held in check for months by a coalition of hostile tribes just beyond their border, but would have destroyed the nest of Sittana fanatics in a week; therefore, it was urged, they should extend our influence transfrontier and gradually absorb the hill-tribes". There was truth in the statement of fact, but not in its corollary. Knowledge was possible without aggression. By degrees the new yeast began to work, and the inert dough gradually rose until an over-aerated loaf was produced in the person of Lord Lytton, whose role was, by tribes, blandishments, or brutality, to quicken reluctant Amir and independent tribes into acceptance of their friendship and protection.

After the departure of Sir Robert Montgomery to England, the Chiefs of the Panjab raised a magnificent memorial in his honour, which took the form of Montgomery Hall, now standing in Lahore, by the side of which bears the name of Sir John Lawrence.

---

1. 16 British and 4 Native.

SIR DONALD McLEOD (1865-1870)

Life Sketch

Sir Robert Montgomery resigned his office on the 10th January, 1865 A.D., and was succeeded in the office of Lieutenant Governor by sir Donald Mcleod. Sir Donald McLeod, (1810-1872), Indian administrator was born at Fort William, Calcutta on May 6, 1810. He was the son of Lieutenant-General Duncan McLeod (1780-1856), Henrietta C.L. Friell, was descended maternally from the French family of Boileau of Castelnau. In 1826 he entered Haileybury, where he became a friend of Sir John Lawrence, and on December 10, 1828 reached Calcutta. For a time he was stationed at Monghyr in Bengal, but in 1831 passed a short time with Sir William Sleeman on the special service created by Lord William Bentinck for the suppression of the 'thugs' and dacoits. He was accordingly appointed in the same year collector and magistratefor Benaras, and in 1849 succeeded Sir John Lawrence as Commissioner of Jullundur, and the Trans-Satluj States.

In 1854 he became Financial Commissioner of the Panjab, and on April 18, 1855 the Court of Directors acknowledged his service to native education in a minute. At Lahore, where he succeeded Edmonstone, he remained there throughout the Mutiny and at its close in 1858 he was created C.B. In 1859 he returned to England. But was back at Lahore the following year. He was President of the Famine Relief Committee in 1861. In January, 1865 he became, by Lawrence's recommendation, Lieutenant-Governor of the Panjab, and was made K.C.S.I. in 1866, and retired in 1870. Returning to England he interested himself in philanthropic movement, and was chairman of the Sindh, Panjab and Delhi Railway. He died on November 28, 1872 in St. George Hospital, London, from the results of an accident on the Metropolitan Railway, and was buried at Kensal Greeen Cemetry.

McLeod was a sincerely religious man but some what dilatory in business matters. Sir John Lawrence knew him well, and used to call him 'the Cunctator.' John Lawrence left an amusing sketch of McLeod's character in a letter (Aug.1, 1853) to Edwardes : 'Morally and intellectually he had no superior in the Panjab, perhaps no equal. But as an administrator he was behind Edmonstone, Raikes, and even Burnes. He was too fond of polishing......He wasted much time on unimportant matters. Donald used to spend half day in writing elegant demi-official chits.' On the other hand, very few administrators had managed, as McLeod managed, to gain the esteem of both natives and Europeans. A portrait of him is at Lahore, and represents the testimonial of the English in the Panjab at the close of his governorship.

Panjab University Lahore

In 1858, the Panjab Government submitted a proposal to the Supreme Government to establish a University at Lahore. After a considerable correspondence, the Government sanctioned the establishment of an instruction to be styled the Lahore University College, with a governing body or senate, consisting of the Lieutenant-Governor of the Panjab on the ground of their being eminent benefactors and original promoters of the institu-tion, or persons distinguished or attainments in Literature or Science.

Powers of the Senate

The Senate so constituted was empowered to expand the income, its disposal in the foundation of fellow-ships and scholarships; in making grants in aid to eductional instituion conducted in accordance with the principles of the movement: granting rewards for vernacular translation of European standard works, and for the encouragement of enlightened study of Oriental Literature: to grant certificates of proficiency after examination to be conducted under rules framed by the Senate on certain accepted principles, the general object of which was to encourage the diffusion of Western literature, as far as possible, through the medium of vernaculars, but where it was not possible through the medium of English.

Further the Senate was to be, with the educational officers of Government, the "Council of Education", or consulting body, in matters relating to education for the province. In support of the institution, Government granted an equivalent to the income from subscriptions and endowments up to Rs. 21,000 per annum.

Lastly, while disallowing for the present, the title of "University" and declining to grant power to confer degrees, the Government intimated its readiness to re-consider this portion of its decision, should the institution prove itself worth of the superior status of a University. The idea of the improvement and extension of vernacular literature generally, and of the encouragement of the enlightened study of the Eastern classical language and literature originated with Sir Donald McLeod, who addressed the Director of Public Instruction on the subject, fully expressing his view as to the development of the scheme. These were communicated by Director for the Anjuman-i-Panjab, a society established at Lahore for the diffusion of useful knowledge under presidency of Dr. Leitner.

That body and its learned president took up the subject warmly, and at many busy meetings which were held by the members, European and Native, and with which were associated many distinguished names (such as Sir Charles Aitchison and Sir James Lyall) the scheme of Sir Donald McLeod developed itself into a University movement.

To carry out the policy of the University College, the Senate established an Oriental School and College at Lahore, endowed lectureships, literary fellowships and scholarships and held public examiniation in various subjects of study which was desired to encourage.

On Feburuary 9, 1870 A.D., Duke of Edinburgh, the second son of Queen Victoria, visited Lahore, and was received by the Lieutenant-Governor, the civil and military authorities and the principal feudatories and chiefs of the province. There was a review of troops at Mianmir, a provincial ball at the Montgomery Hall, and a conversation at Goverment House. The Duke left for Amritsar on February 12, 1870.

In January, 1870 A. D., the five year's term of Sir Donald McLeod having expired, he was asked to remain for a further period of six months. At the conclusion of this period he resigned office on the 1st of June, Sir Henry Marion Durand. succeeded Sir Donald McLeod.

Sir Henry Marion Durand (1870-1871)

Sir Henry Marion Durand (1812-1871) Major-General Royal Engineers K. C. S. I, C. B. was born on November 6, 1812. He was the son of a Cavalry-officer who had served in the Peninsula and at Waterloo. At an early age he was left an orphan, was educated at Leicester School and the East India Company's Military College at

Addiscombe. He received a commission as Second Lieutenant in the Bengal Engineers in June 1828.

Lord Mayo arrived in India, to relieve Sir John Lawrence as Viceroy in 1869. and in May 1870 he appointed Sir Henry Marion Durand, with general approbation, Lieutenant-Governor of the Panjab. In making a tour of the North-West Frontier of his province Durand arrived on the last day of 1870 in the nighbourhood of Tank Chief beside him to visit the town. His 'howdah' was crushed against the roof of the gateway and he was thrown to the ground, his head striking against a wall. He was picked up insensible, and though he recovered consciousness, he died peacefully on January 1, 1871.

Durand was a man of warm affection and great ability, gentle and courteous in manner and deeply religious without cast or bigotry. By nature he was reserved, proud, and sensitive, frequently taking needless offence, while his strongly formed opinions expressed in language equally strong, were apt sometimes to give offence.[1]

1. Dictionary of National Biography, Vol. VI, pp. 246-249

5

Panjab During 1871-1882

Sir Henry Davies 1871-1877

Sir Robert Henry Davies who became the Lieutenant Governor of the Panjab in 1871, was born in 1824. He was the son of Sir David Davies, K. C. H. Physician to William IV, Sir Henry Robert Davies was educated at Charter house and Haileybury. He joined the Indian Civil Service in 1844 and served first in the North-West Province. He served during the Mutiny of 1857, with the troops in the Benares Division and was besieged at Azamgarh. He was appointed Secretary to the Panjab Governrnent in 1859. He became the Financial Commissioner in 1864 and the Chief Commissioner of Oudh 1865-1871. He was made K. C. S. I. in 1874 and C. I. E. in 1877. He acted as the Member of the Council of India from 1885 to 1895. He died on August 23, 1902.[1]

Sir Robert Eyles Egerton 1877-1882

Sir Robert Eyles Egerton, succeeded Sir Robert Henry Davies on the 2nd April, 1877. He was the son of William Egerton and was born in 1827, and was educated at Exter College, Oxford and Haileybury in 1847-1849. He was the I. C. S. man who had served in India. He was the Deputy Commissioner of Lahore during the Mutiny of 1859. He acted as Commissioner at Nagpur in 1869 and again came to the Panjab in 1871 as the Financial Commissioner of Lahore. He worked as the Member of the Governor-General's Legislative Council, from 1871 to 1874.[2]

1. Dictionary of Indian Biography-Buckland, p. 112
2. Dictionary of Indian Biography-Buckland, p. 113

Namdhari Or The Kuka Movement 1871-1872

Early History

The Namdhari sect was founded by Balak Singh of village Hazru in the North-West Frontier Province. Balak Singh (1797-1862) was the son of a goldsmith of village Sarvala in the Attock district; who later shifted his business to Hazru in Campbellpur district. He was Arora of the Batra sub-caste. Balak Singh had been inspired by the sermons of one Jawahar Mal, who preached the virtues of poverty and denounced the rich as godless. Jawahar Mal, known for his piety as Sain Sahib, was the son of Dayal Chand, of village Serai Saleh near Haripur. Dayal Chand or Baba Dayal, is the founder of Nirankari movement. A man of humble origin, he cavilled at the shortcomings of the mighty, and assailed the rites and observances which had corrupted the Sikh way of life. He re-emphasized the Sikh belief in Nirankar-the formless one.[1] Baba Dayal started to expound the Granth and drew large crowds to his centre. He came to be known as "Bhagat". and thereafter his descendants who were of the Kalal caste, styled themselves as "Bhagats."

In 1847, Jawahar Mal opened a centre for divine worship entitled the Jagiasi Abhiasi Ashram. Balak Singh followed suit by exhorting his followers to live a simple life and practise no religious ritual other than repeating God's name or Nam (hence Namdhari). It was Balak Singh's personality more than the substance of his sermons that induced his followers to look upon him as a reincarnation of Guru Gobihd singh. Before Balak Singh died he chose one of his most ardent disciple, Ram Singh as his successor. The headquarters of the Namdharis shifted from Hazru to Ram Singh's village Bhaini in Ludhiana disrict.

Baba Ram Singh 1816-1885

Baba Ram Singh, was born at Bhaini Arayian (now called Bhaini Sahib) 16 miles from Ludhiana, in 1816. It was the 'Basant Panchami' when the house of a carpenter (tarkhan) Jassa Singh and his wife Sada Kaur was blessed with the birth of a child.[2] The first

---

1. The Heritage of the Sikhs-Harbans Singh, p. 129
2. Kukas—The Freedom Fighters of the Panjab-Ahluwalia, p. 40

twenty years of Baba Ram Singh's life were spent at Bhaini his native place, attending to the family business. He was married rather early (as was the prevalent practice then) at the young age of 7 into a family of village Dharaur of the same district. The Baba had two daughters, named Nand Kaur and Daya Kaur.

Ram Singh, like Shivaji, owed a lot to his mother Sada Kaur, who nurtured him in the best spirit and traditions of Sikh religion and history. It was from her that he learnt how to read and write Panjabi in the Gurmukhi script and got his first lessons in the love and appreciation of Gurbani, the sacred literature of the Holy Book. The stories from the lives of the Gurus and Bhaktas that she would so often relate to the children, left an indelible mark on his young and impressionable mind. No wonder that he soon became as regular in the daily religious discipline as his mother was.

When he was about 20, he was prevailed upon by his maternal uncle Kabul Singh, himself a soldier, to get enlisted in the Khalsa army. Entering the military service of Maharaja Ranjit Singh in 1836, he remained in that position till 1845. He was attached to a regiment called after the name of Prince Nau Nihal Singh, a grandson of Ranjit Singh. This period was the most important part of his formative years. The movements of his regiment took him to places far and near all over the state and he came into contact with a much larger number of people,w h ich greatly enriched his experience of men and their affairs.[1]

With his regiment Baba Ram Singh once happened to visit Hazru where he fell under the influence of Balak Singh. He became his disciple and dedicated himself to his mission. For his religious pursuits he had ample time in the army which, towards the end of Ranjit Singh's days, was comparatively free from its more arduous tasks. In the First Anglo-Sikh war, Baba Ram Singh fought against the English at Mudki. He gave up service after the occupation of Lahore.[2]

Bhaini Sahib.

Baba Ram Singh returned to his village, Bhaini which became another important centre like Hazru of the Namdhari faith. After

1. Kuka Movemen t-Fauja Singh Bajwa, pp. 4--5.
2. Kukas-The Freedom Fighters of the Panjab-Ahluwalia, p. 42.

Baba Balak Singh's death, in 1862 the chief responsibility passed on to Baba Ram Singh whose growing influence helped in widening the scope of the movement in the central and eastern Panjab. Because Baba Ram Singh had fully well seen the prevailing moral degeneration amongst the Khalsa. Drinking, plural wives, keeping mistresses, leading a hot life of luxury on the pattern of Muslim Amirs, had become the real character of the enriched Sardars. Moral corruption had set in from all directions. Baits were also being thrown to the army by various leaders in the whirlpool of pernicious politics. Sikh religion had been gripped by monopolists of different sects whose teachings did not agree with the teachings of Nanak. Social evils of Sati, child marriage and infanticide had entered the stronghold of the Khalsa society. The innocent village people had forgotten the message of their Gurus and were visiting Tombs and graves for alleviation of their troubles.[1]

Established Missionary as well as Political Foundation.

An elaborate agency for missionary work was set up. The name of the head in a district-Suba, meaning Governor, had a significant, though remote, political implication.

For the purpose of religious propagation and social uplift, bands of musicians (ragi jathas) were fitted out at Bhaini Sahib and sent in different directions. They had the specific instruction to sing nothing but the hymns of the Holy Granth. The following were some of those bands along with their respective areas of operation:[2]

1. Ragi Jatha Bhai Ditoo and Bhai Fakirya-District Sialkot.
2. Ragi Jatha Bhai Prem Singh and Bhai Kirpal Singh Bhadaur, Malwa.
3. Ragi Jatha Bhai Tara and Bhai Pali of Atari-Manjh. Region.
4. Ragi Jatha Bhai Suba Singh-Doaba.
5. Dhadi Jatha (singers of epics) Bhai Pashaura Singh and Bhai Sant Singh of Talwandi Malya-entire Panjab.

Bhai Khazan Singh, Ratan Singh, Harnam Singh, Sujah Singh and Avtar Singh were the musicians operating at Bhaini Sahib proper and in the immediate neighbourhood.

1. Kuka Movement-Fauja Singh Bajwa, p. 15.
2. Baba Ram Singh-Jaswant Singh Jas p. 17.

Besides the musicians, a number of missionaries were appointed, whose number was raised to twenty-two after Baba Ram Singh was placed under internment in 1863. They were called Subas. With the exception of a few, who were assigned management of the Bhaini Darbar and coordination of the work elsewhere, all those people were allotted separate theatres of operation.[1]

Baba Ram Singh had separate gurdwaras built for his followers. He appointed Subas (governors) as stated above who collected funds which were remitted to Bhaini Sahib. He arranged for training of young men in the use of weapons and built up a paramilitary organisation. The Kukas had their own postal runners to carry secret messages. He abolished all distinction of caste among Sikhs; advocated indiscriminate marriages of all calsses; enjoined the marriage of widows, all which he performed himself; he never took alms himself and prohibited his followers from doing so; enjoined abstinence from liquors and drugs...he exhorted his disciples to be clean and truth telling and it was well that every man carried this staff; and they all did; the Granth was their only accepted inspired volume. The brotherhood might be known by the tie of their turban-Sheeda Pag, by a watch-word, by necklace of knots made in a white woollen cord, to repeat beads and which were worn by all the community.[2]

The movement thus gained a political bias. Its chief inspiration was, in fact, derived from opposition to the foreign rule and everything tending to remind one of it was shunned. English education, mill-made cloth and other imported goods were boycotted. In its advocacy of the use of the Swadeshi, the Kuka movement forestalled, in the sixties of the last century, an important feature of the nationalist struggle under the leadership of Mahatma Gandhi.

Baba Ram Singh's religious discourses began to have a political fervour. When he administered 'pahul', besides the usual sermon delivered on such occasions, Ram Singh spoke of the wickedness of the Sikh princes and landowners; of the assumption of guruship by the Bedi and Sodhi descendants of the gurus; of the wickedness of idolatry and casteism. Despite his criticisms of many Hindu practices, Baba Ram

1. Kuka Movement--Fauja Singh Bajwa, p, 32.
2. Kukas-The Freedom Fighters of the Panjab-Ahluwalia, p. 47-4

Singh became an ardent protector of the cow. He further said "Sodhis, Bedis, Mehants, Brahmins and such like are imposters, as none are gurus except Gobind Singh. Temples of Devi, shiva are a means of extortion, to be held in contempt and never visited. Idols and idol-worships are insulting to God, and will not be forgiven. Converts are allowed to read Gobind Singh's Granth, and no other book.[1]"

Kukas boycotted the Govt. post offices.

Kukas even avoided use of the post offices established by the British and depended upon their own system of postal communication. Messages from their leaders were conveyed with special despatch and alacrity. A fast riding follower would carry the letter to the next village where another Namdhari, setting all other work aside, would at once ride off with it. People left off their meals unfinished to reach forward a message.

Maghi fair at Mukatsar.

Early in 1867, Baba Ram Singh's request to go and visit Muktsar on the sacred day of Maghi was refused by the Government as a result of which he sought permission to hold a fair in his own village on the occasion of Holi. Major Perkins, Superintendent of Police at Ludhiana, was willing to allow, but the Inspector-General wanted to restrict the number of those who might visit Bhaini on that day. Meanwhile Baba Ram Singh decided to celebrate the festival at Anandpur Sahib where Sikhs gathered for this purpose from all over the province. The Lieutenant Governor gave him the permission. High ranking police and civil officers were appointed to watch over the movements of the pilgrims.[2]

Anandpur Sahib

Baba Ram Singh set out in great state. He was accompanied by twenty-one of his Subas on horseback and more than two thousand of his followers on foot, with a large number of drums and banners. Mahant Singh of Keshgarh Gurdawara was adamant that the Kukas must not be admitted into the precincts of Anandpur Later under offici-

---

1. Kukas-The Freedom Fighters of the Panjab-Ahluwalia, p. 47-8.
2. Kuka Movement-Fauja Singh Bajwa, pp. 35, 37

al pressure, the Kukas were allowed to enter the Gurdawara proper under certain condition. The mahant insisted that he would only accept the profered money from the Kuka Guru, but refused to pray him. The visit went off peacefully and Government was led to shedding much of their suspicion. All restrictions upon Baba Ram Singh's freedom were withdrawn.[1]

Kukas Joined the Armies of the Indian Princes

The Government found further grounds of suspicion in some of the Kukas joining the armies of the Indian princes. It was feared that the object of such recruits was to get military training and then return to the Panjab to organize a revolt against the British. Since the Kukas were averse to seeking service with the English, some of them had visited Maharaja Ranbir Singh of Kashmir in 1869 and offered to join the state forces. The Maharaja agreed to raise a new regiment and enlisted about 150 Kukas. But the force was disbanded two years later under pressure of the British Government.

A spirit of fanatical national fervour and religious enthusiasm grew among the Kukas and the personality of Baba Ram Singh became the focal point of a close and well organised order. The prospect was not looked upon with equanimity by the Government, who, after the Mutiny of 1857, had become extra watchful. When, in 1863, Baba Ram Singh wanted to go to Amritsar for Baisakhi celebrations, to which he had invited his followers from all over the Panjab, the civil authority in the State was alarmed. The Lieutenant-Governor charged the Deputy Inspector-General of Police and the Deputy Commissioner of Amritsar to ascertain the real intentions of Baba Ram Singh and his companions. The officials were not in favour of imposing any restrictions, especially on the occasion of a religious fair. But two months later when Kukas announced a meeting to be held at village Khote, in Ferozepore district, prohibitory orders were issued banning all Kuka meetings.[2]

Ram Singh arrived in Amritsar and found the city bristling with police. He was unable to make his proclamation. On his return to Bhaini, he was served with a notice forbidding him to leave the village.

1. Kuka-Movement-Fauja Singh Bajwa, pp. 37-38.
2. A History of the Sikhs Vol. II-Kushwant Singh p. 131

He complained that he had been victimised. "Ram Singh remained under surveillance till the government had assured itself that the Kukas would cause no disturbance".

On the Dussehra festival in the autumn of 1867, Ram Singh visited Amritsar with nearly 3,500 of his followers. He was received with honour at the Hari-mandir and other shrines and baptised over 2,000 Sikhs, including members of some well-to-do families of zamindars. By this time Ram Singh had acquired, perhaps without any voilation on his part, the status of secular chief. He travelled with a body-guard of a soldiers and, like a prince, held court every day.[1]

Their Other Activities.

It was also during this period that many of the Kukas were found digging up graves and other places of superstition. Kuka Dewar Singh was convicted and sentenced to two year's rigorous imprisonment. In the Ludhiana district, a party of 22 Kukas defaced a place of Muslim worship at the village of Chuhpar, Police Station Dehlon. The damage was of rupees one hundred, but the case filed against them failed for want of sufficient evidence. The Deputy Inspector of Police at Dehlon reported that 27 graves had been destroyed at a village named Khuttree Koseh. Four accused were punished with six month's rigorous imprisonment, besides fines.. The destruction of Peer Khana and Muree was also reported at Khanna. The punishment was again 6 months' imprisonment and a fine of Rs. 10. Similar reports also poured in from Amritsar, Jullundur, Gurdaspur, Gujranwala, and Sialkot.[2]

Murder of Butchers at Amritsar 15 June, 1871.

A band of ten Kukas-was shortly afterwards formed to destroy the butchers of Amritsar. Weapons were supplied by Lal Singh, a police constable serving at Amritsar. A 'Hom' ceremony with recitations from 'Chandi Path' was most solemnly gone through in the house of Lehna Singh of Amritsar, at which prayers were offered for the success of the enterprize. And then

1. Kuka Movement-Fauja Singh Bajwa, pp. 78-81.
2. Vide Home-Judicial Progs. 273-284 of August, 1872, 245-58.

between twelve and one O'clock on the night of the 15th June, 1871, a murderous attack was made on the butchers in the slaugter-house, situated outside the Lahori Gate of the Amritsar city. Four men, who were sleeping in front of their houses inside the enclosures, were killed outright and three others were badly wounded. The local authorities were taken completely unawares.[1] The weather conditions being unfavourable, tracking was not possible. Moreover, the blue turban and the steel disc indigenously left behind by the assailants led the investigating authorities astray.[2]

After the police enquiry, the case was sent up to the District Magistrate on the 18th and was by him committed to the Sessions on the 19th August. Four of the accused-Fateh Singh, Beela Singh, Hakim Singh and Lehna Singh-sentenced to be hanged, and two others-Lal Singh and Lehna Singh-to be transported for life. The sentences of death, having been confirmed by the Chief court, were carried out on the 15th September, 1871.[3] It was observed by the government as well as the people that the Kukas who murdered the Muslim butchers were led by Baba Ram Singh and proclaimed by the Baba that they were the army of martyrs, destined to restore the Sikh faith and supremacy in its original purity and integrity.[4]

Butchers at Raikot Murdered-July 15, 1871.

As early as 1856, the Government had permitted the establishment of a slaughterhouse at Raikot,[5] which was located outside the city near a Gurdwara. The Gurdwara was associated with the name of Guru Gobind Singh. The Vultures carried the bones etc. from the slaughter-house, and perched themselves on the temple walls to eat away the carrion. In this way, the purity of the Gurdwara was frequently defiled. The Sikh priests narrated it to some of the Kukas who were on a visit to this Gurdwara.

1. Home Judicial, 29th July 1871, Progs, 45-61 (A)
2. Kuka Movement-Fauja, Singh Bajwa, pp. 78-79
3. Home Judicial February, 1872, Progs, 57-58
4. Home Judicial Progs pp. 273-284, August, 1872
5. 16 miles from Jagraon, 27 miles from Ludhiana and 20 miles from Malerkotla.

On the 15th July, 1871, one month after the murder of Amritsar butchers, the attack was made on the slaughter house of Raikot. Two butchers were killed and seven were injured.[1] But the chief butchers, Ranjha and Buta, both escaped. The assailants escaped into darkness of the night before anybody could come upon them. This being the second happening of its kind and following so close upon the first, the Government were naturally greatly upset. It became a serious problem for the authorities to protect the butchers. However, a special police protection was given to them. For these crimes, eight Kukas were hunged and others sentenced to long terms of imprisonment.[2]

Baba Ram Singh Again Restricted

Having noticed such extreme activities the government re-imposed orders restricting Baba Ram Singh to his village and forbade the assemblage of Kukas at religious festivals all over the province. But Kuka passions had been inflamed, and on the Maghi festival in January 1872, they flocked in the hundred to Bhaini. Speeches were made extolling the heroism of the men who had sacrificed their lives for liberation from the foreign yoke. It was also publicly announced that the time prophesised by the 'Sau Sakhi' for the restoration of Sikh power was at hand. Baba Ram Singh had some difficulty in persuading his followers to return peacefully to their homes. However, one band decided to ignore Baba Ram Singh's advice and they determined to attack Malerkotla, a Muslim State where slaughter of cows was lawfully permitted[3] by Government.

The Kukas felt greatly incensed over these executions especially that of Giani Rattan Singh[4] who had been wrongly implicated in the Raikot murder case. Their temper became defiant and some of them openly preached revenge. The British Government became very vigilant and the Commissioner of Ambala Division prepared

1. "Three people were killed and 9 wounded, 4 of them Seriously" (Kuka Movement-Fauja Singh Bajwa, p. 82)
2. Crown Vs. Fateh Singh and others. Judgement of the Panjab Chief Court, dated 9-9-1871 (Rerference 53) and Crown Vs. Mastan Singh and others. Judgement of the Panjab Chief Court dated 1-8-1871.
3. Kuka Movement-Fauja Singh Bajwa, p. 87
4. Kuka Movemen-Fauja Singh Bajwa, p. 83-84-88

a report charging Kukas with sedition and recommending severe official measures against them, including deportation of their leader Baba Ram Singh.

Meeting at Bhaini Sahib

On the 13th January, 1872 there was a meeting of Kukas at Bhaini Sahib, and a gang of about 250[1] of these, after working themselves up into a state of religious frenzy, started off under the leadership of two Jat Kukas of Sakrowdi, in Patiala territory. The cause of Malerkotla incident was the same, i.e. cow-slaughter. The native Muslim State had offered the same provocation which the authorities in British India had afforded to the Kukas. Secondly, the Kukas were greatly agitated due to the execution of their colleagues at Raikot and Amritsar. Thirdly, they had been greatly inspired by the glorious way in which the 'martyrs' of Raikot and Amritsar had gone to the gallows.

In the second week of January, 1872, they began to collect at the Kuka headquarters, Bhaini Sahib. for the purpose of chalking out a Scheme of revenge against the Muslim officers of Malerkotla, who had shown a keen and revengeful attitude in permitting cow-slaughter before the very eyes of the Hindus and the Sikhs. The occasion was provided by the Maghi Mela when more than 500 persons had already assembled at Bhaini Sahib. Many of the Kukas including their leader Hira Singh, were greatly agitated. They openly declared that they would take revenge for the death of Giani Rattan Singh.[2]

Baba Ram Singh informed the police of their intention to do some mischief, saying that he had no control over them, but it was considered sufficient to see them out of the British territory. They were armed with axes, sticks, and were said to have declared that the town of Malerkotla would be the object of their attack.[3]

Attack on Malaud-January 14, 1872

They went to Pael in Patiala territory without causing any disturbance, and re-appreared next day near to Malaud, the seat of

1. Ludhiana District Gazetteer, p. 29 (1904)
2. Kuka Movement-Fauja Singh Bajwa, pp. 83-87,88
3. Kukas The Freedom Fighters of the Panjab-Ahluwalia, p. 84

Sardar Badan Singh, on which they made a sudden attack with the idea, of getting some arms and money. They also perhaps expected that the Sardar would lead them. In this attack two men were killed on each side and a few wounded, the Kukas, however, succeeded in securing three horses, one gun and one sword. No one joined them anywhere on their march, and they never numbered more than 150 men at the outside.[1]

Malerkotla Attack-January 15, 1872

They next proceeded to Malerkotla, which is nine miles distant from Malaud, and on the morning of the 15th made a sudden attack on the palace of Nawab and treasury of the State; but they were driven off when the Kotla guards had recovered from their surprise, and pursued to 'Rarr' in the erstwhile Patiala State territory where to the number of 68 they surrendered to the Patiala authorities[2].

While the Kukas were near to Rarr village looking after their wounded after the morning's heavy fight and taking stock of the situation they were suddenly over-powered by Niaz Ali, the Naib Nazim of Amargarh. Patiala State, who appeared on the scene at about one O' clock in the afternoon. They were made to surrender their arms and were taken from Rarr to Sher, from where the Naib Nazim had come. The Kukas were 68 in number, Niaz Ali had only small force with him, but he was able to achieve his object with the help of the people of Rarr.[3]

At Malaud and Malerkotla they had killed 10 men and wounded 17, while their own loss had been 9 killed and 38 wounded. On getting news of the attacks on Malaud and Malerkotla, Mr. Cowan, the Deputy Commissioner of Ludhiana started for Malerkotla and telegraphed for troops, which arrived soon after Mr. Cowan executed by blowing from guns at Malerkotla 49 of the captured Namdharis and the others were tried by the Commissioner of Ambala(Mr. Forsyth) and executed on the following day. Thus ended the Kuka outbreak of 1872.[4]

1. Kukas The Freedom Fighters of the Panjab-Ahluwalia, p. 84-85. Kuka Movement-Fauja Singh Bajwa, p. 91
2. Parliamentary Paper East India Kuka Outbreak, 1872.
3. Jind State Records Sangin Munshi Khana, File No. 741
4. History of the Sikhs, Vol. II-Khuswant Singh, p. 135

CRITICISM

If the Kukas ever had any plans for a rising they must have been completely upset by these insane proceedings of a small body of fanatics, rushing about the country armed with sticks and axes. The people of the villages through which they passed appear to have been scared by them, and the inhabitants of Rarr, a village in Malerkotla where they were captured, deserted their houses in a body on the approach of the band. The doctrines of Baba Ram Singh were responsible for what happened. He had become a danger to the State, as similar disturbances might be created at any time by his followers. The Baba was at once deported to Rangoon and remained a State prisoner there till his death in 1885 A.D.

According to another critic the Kuka Movement marked a significant stage in the development of national awareness in the country. In the seventies of the last century when the English were reinstalling themselves in India, it gave them another rude jolt.

The Kukas, nevertheless, more strictly adhere to the puritanical faith of Guru Nanak and Guru Gobind Singh than other Sikhs. Their Gurdwaras are not ostentatious, and their worship is devoid of the elements of idolatory (rich canopies and coverings over the Granth, waving of censers, etc.) which have become common practice in orthodox circles. And the Kukas themselves lead austere lives ; they wear the simplest of clothes and observe a rigid code of conduct ; they are punctilious in attending service in their gurdwaras and in observing the tabus of food, drink, and personal department. They also have a place in the history of the Freedom Movement of India. Ram Singh was the first man to evolve non-cooperation and then use of Swadeshi (indigenous goods) as political weapons. The boycott of British goods, government schools, law courts, and the postal service and the exhortation to wear only hand-spun (khaddar) which Baba Ram Singh propagated in the 1860's were taken up again sixty year later by Mahatma Gandhi[1].

Dr. Fauja Singh Bajwa has concluded that the Kuka Movement was political. Unfortunately circumstances or the times did not favour the freedom fighters to fight-out their freedom against the

1. Heritage of the Sikhs-Harbans Singh, p. 83

foreign rule, since the British power was so strong to be challenged. Dr. Fauja Singh Bajwa writes: "The conclusion, which inescapably follows from the forgoing account, is that of the view that the kuka rising was a political rebellion was almost universally recognised: Douts are sometimes entertained as to whether the attack of Malerkotla was the beginning of the rebellion. Men on the spot assert (and their opinion must be given the due weight) that it was so. A serious limitation of this view is that the attack was not followed up by the kukas. To this the answer is given that some kuka groups were noticed approaching Malerkotla from different directions during those days, but they dared not come nearer and dispersed hearing of the fate of their brethren who had been blown off. It is said that had the incipient rebellion not been nipped in the bud, it would have assumed large proportions. Another reason why the rebellion did not develop was that it was pricipitated by Hira Singh and Lehna Singh before the arrangements for it were complete. This argument not only is advanced by the local authorities, but it also supported by the Kuka tradition and literature. However, even if it is admitted that it was precipitated prematurely, it was still undoubtedly a rebellion which, in the event of success of the first attack on in the absence of the savage massacre of Maler-Kotla, might have spread. But the ultimate result would not have been different from what it was, because the British were yet for too powerful to be shaken[1]."

Prince of Wales Visited Lahore : 1876

On January, 1876, prince of wales visited Lahore. He was received on the platform of the Railway Station by the Lieutenant Governor, the Chief Civil and Militay officials and Europeans. The Prince drove round the city and visited the Lahore fort. In the armoury, at the fort, the Prince saw the weapons employed by the Sikhs. His attention was attracted by a tiny cannon, mounted on revolving frame, which was used as a toy by Maharaja Dalip Singh when he was young. At the desire of the Prince of wales, that tiny cannon was sent to England[2].

---

1. Kuka Movement-Fauja Singh Bajwa, pp. 98-99
2. Lahore Past and Present-Muhammed Baqir, pp. 231-32

Third Period of Panjab Settlements, 1871-1879

The third period of Panjab settlements started in 1871 and ended in 1879. During almost the whole of it Sir James Lyall held the office of Settlment Commissioner, and when he left it, he became Financial Commissioner. He took up the former appointment in November, 1871, and in the same month the first Land Revenue Act, XXXIII of 1871, was passed. Sir Robert Egerton influenced the settlement policy of this period, first as Financial Commissioner, and later as Lieutenant-Governor. He and Sir James Fitz James Stephen, then legal Member of Council, were the joint authors of the Land Revenue Act of 1871. The rules under the Act were framed by Mr. D.G. Barkley under Sir Robert Egerton's supervision and were followed by the former officer's revised edition of Thomson's Directions, which was the text-book of revenue officers in the Panjab till the passing of second Land Revenue Act to 1887.

Settlements Effected During this Period

The setlements which belong to this period fell into four groups; (1) The first regular settlement of the six frontier districts and of Muzzaffargarh; (2)The sevised settlements of the three south-western districts, Multan, Jhang, Montgomery and part of Ferozepore; (3)The revised settlement of Jhelum; (4)The revised settlement of the greater part of old Delhi territory, Rohtak, Gurgaon, Delhi, and a tahsil and a half of Karnal.

Some of these settlements had been begun before the opening of this period, and some were not finished at its close. The work in the districts included in the first two groups, except in the case of Peshawar and Hazara, whose settlements belonged largely to the previous period, was under the control of Mr. Lyall; in the districts of the third and fourth groups the local Commissioners were the supervising officials.[1]

The British Control of The North-West Passes

Its Importance

The history of the British connection with Afghan affairs is closely allied with the question of defence of India, and the North-West Frontier. The general policy adopted by the British government,

1. The Panjab Settlements Manual-Douie, pp. 32-33

was to have the control of Afghanistan and that it should not be allowed to be brought under Russian influence. It was with a view to checkmate. Russian moves in the direction of Central Asia, and Iran; and to avoid embarrassment to the British Indian Government by the extension of any Russian influence in Afghanistan, that England had been jealous of the interposition of a European power in Afghanistan affairs. This danger was then very much reduced by the engagement of Russia with England not to interfere with in Afghanistan of which the boundaries had been defined. The British Government exercised subject to treaty rights recognising Afghanistan as independent Kingdom under the Shah of Afghanistan, undisputed diplomatic control or influence over the Frontier clans or tribes through whose Mountain-Passes there was the least possibility of a foreign army advancing into the trans-Indus Frontier of British India at some distant future, in view of any perturbed conditions in Europe or Asia.[1]

Early History

The Khaiber Political Agency was bounded on the north by the Kabul river and the Safed-Koh; on the east by Peshawar District; on the south by the Aka Khel and Orakzai countries and on the west by the Chamkanni and Masuzai countries, and the Safed Koh. The Khaiber Pass between Jamrud and Landi Kotal originally belonged to the Shinwaris, Zakka Khel, Kuki Khel, and Orakzai only. At the time of the extension of Sikh rule to Jamrud the Orakzai were ousted by the Afridis, and the only trace of their presence was a ruined village near Jam. The Sikh rule never extended beyond Jamrud. When Colonel Mackeson was negotiating with the Afridis in 1840, the Malikdin Khel Maliks of Chora forced their way between the Zakka Khel and Kuki Khel, and established a small village at Katta Kushta near Ali Masjid. The Sipah Kambar Khel and Kamrai Khel also, seeing the advantages of footing in the Khaiber, stepped in, and were admitted to a share in the Khaiber allowance.

Afridis Joined The British Army

After t. ˬ Sikh War the Afridis took service in large numbers in the British army, and when the Mutiny of 1857 broke out they did exceedingly well. From 1857 to 1878 the Afridis were subsidized by

1. The Evolution of N.W. Frontier Province-D.C. Oberai, pp. 45-46

the Afghan government who kept a garrison of Afghan troops at Ali Masjid. The Afridis were, however. never on good terms with Afghans. They very often visited the British officer of Peshawar District; but relations with them were maintained through the Khalil and Mohmand Arbabs of Peshawar District, who were generally on an intriguing disposition, and very seldom did any real service. Their main object was to keep those tribes in a state of unrest, and thus enhanced their own importance. A year or two before the second Afghan War Amir Sher Ali summoned the 'jirgas', of all the Afridis and Shinwaris, and distributed about 5000 rifles among them. When war broke out, and Ali Masjid was attacked, the Afghans and Afridis fled in great disorder, and the Afghans were robbed of their clothes and rifles by the Afridis in the Khaiber and in Bazar. The Afridis, and especially the Bazar Zakka Khel, subsequently harassed the passage of the British troops through the Khaiber, and a force was sent against them in December, 1878. On the second day of the campaign the fortress of Ali Masjid was brilliantly captured by the British troops under General Browne. The successful passage of the Khaiber, and the unopposed occupation, first of Dakka at the western mouth of the pass, and then of Jalalabad in the plains beyond, immediately followed. The treaty which closed the war in May, 1879, left the Khaiber tribes for the future under British control. From that date the history of the Khaiber Pass is bound up with that of the Khaiber Political Agency, which included Mullagori country north of the Khaiber, Tirath of the Afridis, and the country on both sides of the Khaiber Pass.

Treaty of Gandmak 1879 A. D.

By the Gandamak Treaty of 1879 between the British and Amir Yakub khan, it was agreed that the British Government should retain the control of the Khaiber Pass: and, in pursuance of this agreement, allowances were fixed for the Afridis, aggregating Rs. 87,540 per annum. The management of the pass was entrusted to the tribesmen themselves through their Maliks, who executed a formal agreement by which they undertook to guard it with their tribesmen. Some local levies called jezailchis,[1] numbering about 400 men, were also raised

1. Whihc afterwards became the Khaiber Rifles

for escorting caravans through the Khaiber. These were evantually increased to 600 strong.[1]

Achievements of the British

Meanwhile, the treaty of Gandamak with Afghanistan and political arrangements with border tribes, secured territorial rights to the British respecting two milltary routes from India to Kabul, namely, the one by the Khaiber and the other by the Kurram, and the British troops were kept in position at Peshawar, Nowshera, Risalpur, Landikotal, Kurram, etc, places wherefrom they could move to those passes at the shortest notice. The British had opened up the tribal areas, in parts, penetrating to posts at Wana, Razmak, Miranshah, Parachinar and Landikotal, by means of motor roads, and establishing military stations. "Province has blessed us with a strong line of Frontier, covered by rugged and harren hills, through which there are but a limited number of passes by army could approach India and the military art teaches us that the best position for the defence of such ground is on our own side of the passes, just where an army must debouch on the plain with Peshawar, Kohat and Sindh, in our possession, and the communications with our Indian Provinces open by rail and steamers on the Indus, and strong force of Europeans located in healthy Cantonments all over the country supported by a well-organised native army, "I consider that we should really have the keys of India in our own pockets, be in a position to lock the doors in the face of all enemies black or white."[2]

A chain of picket posts and block houses with forts in suitable places completes the defence of North-West Frontier Province against any land forces from the west, and amongst recent more advanced defence measures, is the provision of antiaircraft guns, in sufficiently large numbers, for effective defence against any possible attack from the air. This is an aspect in evolution of North-West Frontier Province, the importance of which cannot be overrated.[3]

1. Imperial Gazetteer, North-West Frontier province pp. 230-232
2. Sir Henry Lumsden wrote in his Report on the Kandhar Mission.
3. The Evolution of N.W. Frontier Province-D.C. Oberai, p. 46

The Peasants In Prosperity And Debt

The reclamation of desert lands by the extension of canal irrigation, combined with facilities for marketing agricultural produce, ushered in an era of prosperity that the Panjab had never seen. But this prosperity brought in its wake other economic changes which radically the social fabric of life in the Panjab. The direct consequence of the increrse in the earning from agriculture was the increase in the price of land; it rose from a mere Rs. 10/- per acre in 1870 to more than Rs. 100/- per acre by the turn of the century.[1] The land became a valuable commodity, and small farmers were unable to resist the temptation to sell their holdings.[2]

The number of landless farmers assumed alarming proportions. The famine of 1869[3] attended by heavy mortality of livestock accentuated the problem. Agriculturists were unable to pay revenue due from them and were compelled to borrow. Then Ushered an era in 1870 of the Peasants of the Panjab's indebtedness which had never been known in the country before. From 1877, which was another year of serious shortage-it assumed alarming proportions. The elaborate legal system introduced by the British contributed much towards the impoverishment of the peasantry and the encirclement of money-lenders and lawyers.

The process had begun in 1859 when three years were fixed, as the limitation of all debts unprotected by registered bond-thus forcing creditors to hurry to courts. The introduction of Civil procedure Code, the setting up of the Chief Court at Lahore in 1866, the passing of the Evidence Act and Contract Act, in 1872, gave indigenous lawyers and their clients[4] opportunities to prolong litigation. The straw that broke the back of the peasantry was the creation in 1874-75, of Munsiff's Courts to try debt disputes. Till then District Officers with close knowledge of the peasant's problems and revenue matters had dealt with these disputes simply cheaply and equitably. The Munsiffs, largely urbanites ignorant of rural affairs, proved to be harsh and often corrupt.[5]

---

1. The Wealth & Welfare of Panjab-Calvert, p. 219
2. Report on Peasant Indebtedness and Land Alienation-Thorburn, p. 10
3. The Panjab Peasant in Prosperity, and Debt-Darling, p. 97
4. In this money lenders could afford them more than agriculturists.
5. Report on Peasant Indebtedness and Land Alienations-Thorburn p. 47.

Besides the events described above, on the 1st of January, 1877, Queen Victoria's assumption of the title of Empress of India (Qaisar-i-Hind) was announced at great Darbar at Delhi. In 1877 Kashmir hitherto controlled by the Lieutenant-Governor, was put directly under the Government of India. The same year and the next the Province was tried by famine an account of which has already been given.

6

Punjab During 1882-1892

(Sir Charles Atichison 1882-1887)

Early Life

Sir Charles Umpherston Atichison (1832-1896), Lieutenant Governer of the Panjab, was born in Edinburgh on May 20, 1832. He was the son of Hugh Aitchison of that city, by his wife Elizabeth, daughter of Charles Umpherston of Loanhead near Edinburgh, and was educated in the high School and University, where he took the degree of M. A. on April 23, 1853. While a student in the University of Edinburg, Aitchison attended the lectures of Sir William Hamilton (1788-1856).

Under Secretary

In 1859 he joined the Secretariat of the Government of India as Under-Secretary in the Political Department, and served there until 1865, when, at the instance of Sir John Lawrence, then Governor-General, he took up administrative work in the Panjab, serving first as a Deputy Commissioner and subsequently officiating as Commissioner of Lahore. In 1868 he rejoined the Secretariat as Foreign Secretary, and retained that appointment until 1878.

Pro-Indians

He became Lieutenant-Governor of the Panjab on April 4, 1882. He was a staunch advocate of policy of advancing natives of India in the public service as they proved their fitness for higher post and for more responsible duties. On this point, in connection with what is known as the Ilbert Bill, he advocated measures even more liberal than those proposed by Lord Ripon's government. He had intended to leave India for good when his Lieutenant-Governorship came to an end in 1887, but being invited by Lord Dufferin to join the Governor-General and give the Viceroy the benefit of his experience on many questions which had to be dealt with consequent upon the annexation of Upper Burma, he returned to India for another nineteen months.

During the latter part of his government of the Panjab he had discharged the additional duty of presiding over the Public Service Commission, and this duty he continued to perform after joining the Governor-General's Council. He retired and finally left India in November, 1888. Early in the following year he settled in London, but subsequently moved to Oxford.

A Religious Man

Aitchison, an essentially religious man, was a consistent and warn supporter of Christian Missions while in India, and after his retirement was an active member of the Committee of the Church Missionary Society. He died at Oxford on February 18, 1896.[1]

A Great Administrator

"He had a splendid record of service dating back to the Mutiny year, and intellectually was one of the most gifted civilians of his generation. But he had not the complete confidence of the rank and file, partly because he had made his name more as Secretary than as an administrator and partly because he was closely identified with Lord Ripon's radical schemes of reform which many regarded as premature".[2]

There was then an easy feeling that the Secretariat was gaining an under influence and that skill in minute writing rather than capacity of administration was the test of efficiency and the stepping-stone to promotion. Any how the appointment of Sir James Lyall to succeed Aitchison in the spring of 1887 was gonerally welcomed by the official world and the rural interests.

---

1. The Dictionary of National Biography, Vol. XXII, pp. 25-26.
2. India as I knew it-O'Dwyer, pp. 28-29.

SIR JAMES BROADWOOD LYALL-1887-1892

Early Life

Sir Charles Aitchison was succeeded by Sir James Broadwood Lyall on April 2, 1887. Sir James Broadwood was born on Macrh 6, 1838 and was the son of Rev. Alfred Lyall. He was educated at Eton and Haileybury. He joined the Bengal Civil Service and was posted in the Panjab in 1858-59, as the Financial Commissioner. He acted as the Resident in Mysore, 1883-87. After the Lieutenant-Governorship of the Panjab he was appointed the Member of the Royal Opium Commission in 1893-94, and the President of the Indian Famine Commission in 1898. He was made K.C.S.I. in 1888 and G.C.S.I., in 1892.[1]

Sir James Broadwood Lyall held the office of Financial Commissioner since 1879. He was transferred from the Panjab to a higher appointment. His ripe experience and intimate knowledge of the people and of their requirements were a source of strength to the Administration, and the member in which he conducted the onerous duties of the office were highly appreciated by the government.[2]

The period from 1882 to 1892 was one of quiet development. The Sirhind Canal was opened in 1882, and the Weir at Khanki for the supply of the Lower Chenab Canal was finished in 1892. A detailed account of this Canal system has been given in a separate chapter. New Railways were constructed and Lord Ripon's Policy of Local Self-Government found a strong supports in Sir Aitchison, and Acts were passed dealing with the constitution and powers of Municipal Committees and District Boards. Account of the Municipal Committees and District Boards has been discussed separately. In 1884 and 1885 a large measures of reorganisation was carried out. A separate staff of Divisional, District and subordinate Civil Judge was appointed.

The Deputy Commissioner henceforth was a Revenue Collector and District Magistrate with large powers in criminal cases. The Revenue adminstration was at the same time being improved by the

1. Dictionary of Indian Biography-Buckland, p. 214.
2. Panjab Administration Report, 1882-1883.

reforms embodied in the Panjab Land Revenue and Tenancy Acts passed at the beginning of Sir James Lyall's administration. A brief account of the Legislation work done during this period is given below :—

COURSE OF LEGISLATION

In reviewing the various former Acts, Regulations and Rules which had been extended to the Panjab Province during the period under study, can be conveniently divided into the following classes :—

- I Acts affecting the Panjab in common with other Provinces of British India.
- II Acts passed specially for the Panjab.
- III Frontier Regulations.
- IV Rules having the force of law.

I. Acts Affecting The Panjab In common with other Provinces

In this class the principal measures introduced were as follows :—

1. In the year 1883-84 Acts No.XIX of 1883 and No.III of 1884 came into force. The former of these, known as the Land Improvement Loan Act, was passed for the purpose of enabling Government to facilitate the lending of money to agriculturists on easy terms with a view to affecting improvements in their holdings.

2. The second amended the Code of Criminal Procedure so far as related to the exercise of jurisdiction over European British subjects.

3. In the year 1884-85 Act XII of 1884, the Agriculturists Loans Act, was extended to the Panjab. This Act had in view the prevention of agricultural distress by enabling peasants in times of scarcity to take advances from Government wherewith to buy seed and cattle.

4. In the year 1885-86 several Acts were passed, the most important of which was Act II of 1886. This, which was known as the Income Tax Act, was enacted to enable Government to impose a tax on incomes derived from sources other than agriculture.

5. In the year 1889-90 the Cantonments Act, XIII of 1889, the Indian Railways Act, IV of 1890, and an act to prevent Cruelty to Animals, XI of 1890, came into force.

II. Acts Passed Specially For The Panjab.

In regard to this class, this period is one of considerable interest, many Acts having been passed which dealt with various subjects of importance to this Province.

1. In the year 1883-84 the District Boards Act, XX of 1883, superseded the old Local Rates Act of 1878.

2. In 1884-85 were passed the Panjab Municipal Act, XIII of 1884 and the Panjab Courts Act, XVIII of 1884. The District Boards Act of 1883 and the Municipal Act of this year formed part of the various measures which had been taken to extend the function of Local Bodies, in connection with the development of Local Self-Government, and the Panjab Courts Act was required to give effect to the scheme for the re-organisation of the Civil Administration of the Panjab.

3. Tenancy & Land Revenue Acts

In the year 1887-88 the two most important Acts of the period came into force, viz, the Panjab Tenancy and Land Revenue Acts, XVI, and XVII of 1887. These Acts were the fruition of long and careful deliberation. The Tenancy Act, which superseded Act XXVIII of 1868, did not involve any great departure from the principles and policy of the Act of 1868, but was enacted mainly to supply some admitted oversights and defects, and to adopt some of the suggestions made by the Famine Commission with a view to improving the relations of landlords and tenants generally. These relations had become very strained in certain districts of the Panjab, especially Sirsa and Hoshiarpur. In the former of these districts the landlords had commenced to resort very largely to eviction to prevent the growth of occupancy rights, while in Hoshiarpur the uncertainty of the law as to enhancement of rent threatened the district with an immense flood of litigation on the conclusion of the operations of settlement Apart from the circumsta- nces of these districts, the law required modification for the purpose of removing ambiguities and correcting certain omiss-ions or mistakes and affording protection to tenants whose successors in interest would have enjoyed this or who had earned a right to special consideration by breaking up waste land. The main changes of the new Act were as follows:-

1. Original settlers were placed in as good a position with reference to

occupancy right as successors of original settlers were by the former Act.

2. Reverting to the practice in force before 1868, the scale fixed for enhancement and reduction of rents of occupancy tenants would be adjusted with reference to the land revenue instead of with reference to the rents paid by tenants at will in the same or adjacent estates. The uncertainty of the latter method of adjustment had given rise to wide spread litigation.

3. Power was given to Settlement Officers to determine the rents of occupancy tenants at the time of the assessment of land revenue when such rents were expressed in terms of the land revenue.

4. The provision for the payment of compensation for improvements were made liberal, and reclamation and clearing tenants were allowed compensation on ejectment from the lands they had brought under cultivation.

5. The saving force of Section 2 of the Act of 1868 in regard to agreements made between landlord and tenants had been somewhat restricted, and on grounds of policy the provisions of the Act had been made to prevail over such agreements made subsequent to its passing.

The Land Revenue Act replaced an Act incomplete in many respects and combrous in others, and under the policy of Government in insiting on the careful maintenance of village records could be carried out only with difficulty. Its re-enactment was finally rendered imperative by an attempt to revise the large body of rules which had issued its authority, when technical difficulties arose which made a new Act a matter of necessity[1].

In the case of waste, adjoining an estate, if the record-of-rights of the estate was completed before 18th November, 1871, and did not specifically say that the waste belonged to the estate, the presumption was that it belonged to the British Government. And in the records-of-rights after that date, where it was not specifically said that the waste belong to Government, it was presumed to belong to the estate: the presumption might be rebuted on certain grounds stated in subsection (3) of Section 42.

1. Panjab Administration Report 1892-93, pp. 115-117.

The Act also continued the provision about 'excess waste,' which had usually found place in Revenue Acts (cf Section 87, Act XIX of 1873, and p. 37). Even if the waste had been granted to an estate, it might be in excess of requirements, and then a portion might be marked off and separately assessed. The Settlement must, however, be offered to the holders of the original estate, and only, if they refused it, to others; in that case, an allowance of 10 per cent, as a maximum, and 5 per centas a minimum of the net income realized by Government, was given to the original estate-owners. No Civil Court had jurisdiction to hear any suit regarding the 'formation of an estate' out of waste land.

IMPROVEMENT AND COLONISATION OF WASTE

Even after the allotment, there were districts is which great tracts of land still remained for disposal by the State; and these were often such as were not in demand, because 'barani' cultivation-depending on rainfall, was impossible, and the land was so near the 'bar' that wells could not profitably be sunk. Yet the soil was good. Of late year, the Chenab Canal had made possible the cultivation of a large tract of this kind in the Rechna Doab (Gujranwala and Jhang Districts), and the recently-constructed Sidhnai Canal (from the Ravi) had done the same for the northern part of the Multan district; and so with the Para and Lower Sohag Canals (extensions of the Upper Satluj Canal) in the Montgomery district.

It had become a recognized part of land-revenue administration to manage, on a regular system, the allotment and colonization of these new canal lands. This was over and above the ordinary system of disposing, by lease of waste lands available in the districts generally.

Ordinary Waste Land Rules.

The principles on which the rules were framed were; that the Government, in the first instance, leased, and did not sell, the land; it charged a low rate of land-revenue and also took a rent (for malikana), which amounted to one-fourth of the revenue. No lease was allowed without the sanction of the Government, except in eight districts (Montgomery, Jhang, Multan, Shahpur. the two Derajat districts, Muzaffargarh and Bannu), and even there, leased of over 3000 acres require sanction; and so if the lessee proposes to make a canal, or if Government was likely to make one in the neighbourhood. During the currency of the lease, the 'malikana' might be redeemed or compounded for, on payment of twenty-five years' dues. When that was done, the proprietary title to the land was acquired, and the purchaser would have in future only to pay (like any other proprietor) the assessed land-revenue to his estate.[1]

PANJDEH INCIDENT-1884

Complicated Position

The chief dispute centered round **Panjdeh**, a village and district, one hundred miles due south of Merv where the Murghab and Kushak rivers unite their waters. The whole position was complicated and difficult. The Commissioners were sub-ordinate to the Foreign Offices of London and St. Peterburg respectively and neither the Government of India nor the Russian Governor-General of Turkistan had direct control over them.

Panjdeh is the famous incident which brought Russia and Great Britain on the brink of war. In 1881, the Russians annexed Merv, which caused great anxiety in the mind of the Government of India and that of Great Britain. A Commission was appointed to fix the northern boundary line of Afghanistan. A difficulty arose with regard to the position of Panjdeh which was under the Afghan rule. The Russian General ordered the Afghans to leave Panjdeh and when the order was not carried out he drove the Afghans away forcibly.

Shrewed Commonsense of the Amir

Finding the situation serious, the **Indian armies** were assembled at Quetta and the Russian armies at **Herat**. However, the disastrous issue of war was averted by the labours of diplomatists, the tact of Lord Dufferin and above all by the shrewed commensense of Abdur Rahman. He declared that he was not sure whether Panjdeh belonged to him or not and he was also not very desirous of keeping the same in his possession. The Amir further declared his willingness to give up his claim to Panjdeh if he was given compensation anywhere else.

1. The Land System of British India, Vol. II-Baden Powell pp. 548-550

Abdur Rahman Saved Afghanistan

The Amir was determined to avoid a clash between Great Britain and Russia. He knew fully well that in the event of a war between the two, his country was to suffer because it was to become the theatre of war. Abdur Rahman rightly pointed out that "Afghanistan was between two mill-stones and it had been already ground to powder." To quote Abdur Rahman again, "My country is like a poor goat on whom the lion and the bear have both fixed their eyes and without the protection and help of Almighty Deliverer the victim cannot escape very long."

Meeting at Rawalpindi

Lord Dufferin's conference with the Amir of Afghanistan at Rawal-Pindi in 1885 did much to strengthen the latter's good-will to the British. The personal charm and tact of the Viceroy exerted much the same influence over Abdur Rahman as that of Lord Mayo had done over his predecessor Sher Ali, but again it was made clear that the reigning Amir was just as determined as his predecessor had ever been to exclude, at all hazards, British troops and officers from Afghanistan. Lord Dufferin criticized the weakness of the fortifications of Herat and proposed to send English Royal Engineers to strengthen them; but against this suggestion Abdur Rahman was obdurate on the ground that the Afghan would at once imagine that their independence was being attacked, and that mischief would result. Fortunately Lord Dufferin showed greater readiness than Lord Lytton to appreciate the Afghan point of view, and he refrained from pressing his suggestion recognizing that this intense jealousy for their national integrity would inspire the Afghans with bitter enmity against any people seeking to make their country a base for the invasion of India. Abdur Rahman left the conference gratified with the honours paid to him, impressed by the evidences of India's military strength and with sentiments of warm friendship for the Viceroy[1].

1. History of British India-P.E. Roberts, pp. 476-77

Boundary Line Demarcated

Accordingly, though Sir Peter Lumsden had been recalled, Sir West Ridgeway continued his labours. The joint commission after long negotiations agreed upon a frontier line from the Hari Rud over the spurs of the Paropamisus range to the low ground of the Oxus valley, but they were unable to come to a satisfactory understadding as to the exact point where the line should touch the Oxus. Sir West Ridgeway, after visiting the Amir at Kabul and discussing the matter with Lord Dufferin at Simla, proceeded to England. Finally, after prolonged negotiations between Kabul, Simla, London, and St. Peterburg, the line of demarcation was settled by a protocol signed at St. Petersburg in July 1887.

What had been accomplished was of very considerable importance. Sir West Ridgeway declared that by the new boundary the Amir did not lose a penny of revenue, a single subject, or an acre of land. The settlement of the frontier up to the line of the Oxus put definite limits to the Russian advance in the direction of Herat, which strategists had agreed to look upon as the key of India.[1] Farther east in the direction of the Pamirs the Russian forward movement still continued until, as we shall see another Anglo-Russian convention was signed in 1895.

THE BRITISH AGENT AT GILGIT

Geographical Situation of Gilgit

The country of Astor is reached where the Gilgit road from Kashmir descends from the Burzil pass.[2] It was drained by the Astor river, which joins the Indus to the south of Bunji. The bridge which crossed it at at Ramghat was only 3800 feet above sea level. The village of Astor itself was at a height of 7,853 feet. The cultivation is of the same description as that in Baltistan. The aspect of the country was bleak till the Indus is crossed, and Gilgit[3] was reached. Here there was a fertile well-watered oasis from which on every side great mountain peaks were visible. The lands were heavily manured. Rice, Maize, millet, buck-wheat,

1. History of British India, p. E. Roberts, p. 476
2. 13,500 feet
3. 4890 feet

cotton, wheat, barley, grapes and lucerne were grown. There was a second and easier road to Gilgit from India over the Babusar pass at the top of the Kagan Glen in Hazara. But the posts were sent by the Kashmir road.[1]

Historical Importance :

The real importance of Gilgit to the British Government was that it gave direct communication with Chitral, a small state with an area "rather larger than that of Wales" and population of about eighty thousand, hardly mountaineers, which commanded the easiest and least elevated passes across the Hindu-Koh.[2] Chitral, the Pathan country ended the Lowari pass. Beyond, right up to the main axis of the Hindu-Koh, is Chitral. It comprised the basin of the Yarkhun or Chitral river from its distant source in Shawar-Shur glacier to Arnawai, where it receives from the west, the waters of the Bashgul, and was thence forth known as the Kunar. Its western boundary was the Durand Line, which followed a lofty chain sometimes called the Kafiristan range.[3]

British Forward PoLicy

Throughout the nineties of the nineteenth century, especially from 1878 onwards, these districts of the North West Frontier were abnormally disturbed. There were two main reasons for this :

1. The forward policy pursued under Lord Lansdowne and Lord Elgin, and

2. The intrigues of the Amir of Afghanistan.

By the year of 1889 Sandeman had extended British control over the Bori and Zhob valleys, to the south of the Gomal[4] pass. The occupation of Zhob was of paramount importance from a military, political and commercial stand point. Not only did it shorten the British line of defence and prevented raiding gangs from escaping into Afghanistan, but it also served as protection for the Gomal trade route. In the year

1. The Panjab N.W.F. & Kashmir-Douie, p. 321.
2. The Panjab, N.W.F. & Kashmir-Douie, p. 307.
3. History of British India-P.E. Roberts, p. 491.
4. The Panjab, N.W.F. & Kashmir-Douie. pp. 25, 312.

1890 the Gomal river, from Domandi to its junction with the Zhob stream, was declared the boundary between Balochistan and the Panjab frontier zone.

Anglo-Afghan Relations Strained

The opening years of the nineties witnessed punitive expeditions against the Shiranis inhabiting the slopes of the Takht-i-Sulai-man[1]: the Orakzai clans in the neighbourhood of the Samana range; the Isazai tribes of the ill-omened Black Mountain;[2] and the pettys chiefs, of Hunza of Nagar. Far more important, than these petty wars was the peaceful acquisition of the Kurram valley, which was taken over, in 1892, at the request of its Turi inhabitants. This active policy along the entire length of the British border, especially its later developments, not only alarmed the tribesmen but it also alarmed Abdur Rahman Khan, with the result that, between 1890 and 1898, Anglo-Afghan relations were so strained that on several occasions war seemed imminent.

The Same Racial Stock

When it was realised that the inhabitants of the frontier Hills, were orthodox Muslims of the Sunni sect, and were, in many cases, of the same racial stock as the people of south-eastern Afghanistan, it became apparent that Abdur Rahman was able to show his displeasure by exploiting the marauding proclivities of the turbulent tribesmen. For this reason, it was fortunate for the British during the Mutiny that diplomatic negotiations had resulted in the Anglo-Afghan Treaty of 1855 and the Agreement of January, 1857.

The outbreak war with Afghanistan in 1878 was the signal for increased disturbances throughout the tribal zone. The Hazara border was in a perpetual ferment; the Khaiber was constantly raided by Zakka Khels and Mohmands; Zaimushta harassed the Kohat line of communication; and Mahsuds from the heart of Waziristan raided and laid waste the country in the vicinity of Tank.

---

1. The Panjab, N.W.F. & Kashmir-Douie. pp. 26, 318.
2. Expedition against Isazi clans-Mason Parl. Papers, 1890-1.

Amir Abdur Rahman warned the Viceroy

For some time before despatch of the Durand Mission to Kabul, in 1893, it had been rumoured that the British were desirous of a more exact delimitation of the Indo-Afghan Frontier. This might had led to the increase of the Amir's intrigues in Zhob and Waziristan. It undoubtedly prompted Abdur Rahman Khan to write a letter to the Viceroy in which he warned Lord Lansdowne of the results of a more forward policy.

"If you should cut them out of my dominions", he wrote, "they will neither be of any use to you nor to me. You will always be engaged in fighting or other trouble with them, and they will always go on plundering. As long as your government is strong and in peace, you will be able to keep them quiet by a strong hand, but if at any time a foreign enemy appears on the borders of India, these frontier tribes will be your worst enemies...In your cutting away from me these frontier tribes, who are people of my nationality and my religion, you will injure my prestjge in the eyes of my subjects, and will make me weak, and my weakness is injurious for your government.[1]"

Durand Line :

By the terms of the treaty of Gandamak, limits of the Afghan sphere of influence were set back along the main lines between India and Kabul to the western ends of the Khaiber Pass and the Kurram Valley, but on the north and south of these routes no boundary was fixed. At intervals during their history some measure of control has been exercised over the Pathan tribes from Kabul, and the more important of them, such as the Afridis, and Mohmands, had been in receipt of allowances from Amir Abdur Rahman for keeping open the passes. But practically they had been independent and their main object had always been to remain so.

In 1893 the Amir consented to a precise fixing of boundries, and a mission, under Sir Mortimer Durand, proceeded to Kabul to discuss the question. An ageeement was signed definitely fixing the line which the Government of India and the Amir had agreed to regard as the

1. Autobiography-Abdur Rahman, p. 11.

frontier of Afghanistan from Chandak,[1] to the Persian border., Commissions were next issued to demarcate the boundary. The Asmar Commission (1894) demarcated from the Bashgal valley on the borders of Kafiristan to Nawa Kotal, a point on-the confines of Bajaur and the Mohmand country. This delimitation was accepted by both governments but south of the Nawa Kotal no demarcation was made, owing to disagreement, the Amir being unwilling to admit the boundary framed by the Durand agreement in the Mohmand territory, Between the Kabul river and Sikaram[2] no demarcation was attempted. But in the same year (1894) boundary stones were set up on the Kurram border, and orders were issued for demarcation from the Kurram to the Gomal river, which led to the Mahsud expedition. In 1895 this demarcation was carried out, after which no further work on the boundary was undertaken.

Not based on Sound Topographical Data

The new boundary line was not based upon sound topographical data, for during the process of demarcation, it was discovered that certain places, marked on the Durand map, did not exist cn the actual ground. Many ethnic absurdities were perpetrated, such as the handing over to the Amir of the Birmal tract of Waziristan, peopled by Darwesh Khel Waziris, the majority of whom were included within the British sphere of influence. The worst blunder of all was the arrangement by which the boundary cut the Mohmand tribal area into two separate parts. It was certain that that could not have been a tripartite agreement, for there was no evidence that the tribesmen were consulted.[3]

In the light of subsequent events it is difficult to understand the reasons which prompted the Amir to sign this agreement. It might have been that the increase of his subsidy to eighteen lakhs of ruppes, and the recognition of his right to import munitions of war, bribed him into acquiescence.

---

1. In the valley of the Kunar river, 12 miles north of Asmar.
2. Safed-Koh.
3. Cambridge History of India, Vol. VI, p. 462

Fratricidal Conflicts and Chitral

Equally important is the Chitral incident. While these negotiations were taking place Chitral became the scene of fratricidal conflicts. On his death, in 1892, Aman-ul-Mulk, the Mehtar of Chitral, had been succeeded by one of his sons, Afzal Mulk, who, after a short reign of two months and seven days, was slain by his uncle, Sher Afzal, who had been allowed to escape from Kabul where he had been living as a pensioner of the Amir. Sher Afzal held the reins of government until he was ousted from his nephew, Nizamal Mulk who was recognised by the Government of India. It was significant that Sher Afzal fled to the camp of the Afghan Commander-in-Chief at Asmar.[1]

A Mission to Chitral

In answer to the new Mehtar's request, a mission under Dr. Robertson was despatched to Chitral. Although Robertson advocated the retention of British troops in Chitral and Yassin, Lord Lansdowne, towards the end of 1893, issued instructions for the withdrawal of the political officer from Chitral, if no further complications occurred. Two factors were instrumental in reversing this decision.

1. It was considered inexpedient to withdraw so long as the Pamir boundary dispute with Iran afforded an excuse for aggressive action from that direction.

2. It was feared that, owing to the hostile attitude of Umra Khan of Jandol, on the southern borders of Chitral, withdrawal would be followed by a period of anarchy,

Mehtar Murdered

In January, 1895, the Mehtar was murdered, and Sher Afzal once more appeared on the scene. To make matters worse, Umra Khan proclaimed a 'Jehad' throughout Dir, Swat, and Bajaur. and Robertson found himself besieged in the Fort of Chitral by a combined force of Chitralis and Pathans. This necessitated the immediate despatch of a relief column. The memorable siege from 4 March to 19 April, 1895; the heroic efforts of the defenders; Kelly's marvellous march of 350 miles in 35 days from Gilgit; and the advance of Sir

1. Forward Policy and Ist Results-Bruce, p. 141

Robert Low by way of the Malakand were well known to students of history of the frontier problem.[1]

Prior to Low's march over the Malakand, the only communication with Chitral was by way of Kashmir and the isolated position of Gilgit. Not only was this route circuitous and the roads bad, but Gilgit for many months in the year was cut off by snow from both India and Chitral. The question of the retention of a garrison in Chitral, therefore, hinged on the proposal to construct a more direct road over the Malakand. As soon as it had been decided to move troops over the Malakand and Lowarai to Chitral, a proclamation had been issued on 14th March, 1895, to the pepole of Swat and Bajaur, to the effect that if they granted British forces an umolested passage through their terreitories their country would not be occupied. On 8 May 1895, the Government of India decided to retain a garrison in Chitral; and, to, ensure its safety, proposed the construction of a road from Peshawar through Swat.

Necessity of Retention of Garrison In Chitral

Was the retention of a garrison in Chitral a strategic necessity for the protection of the frontier? It was pointed out at the time that, by the Durand Agreement, the Amir had pledged himself not to interfere in Swat, Bajaur, or Chitral: consequently all danger from Afghanistan had passed away. On the other hand, the Afghan intrigues had played no small part in the recent struggles in Chitral. On 10 September 1895, the Pamir boundary dispute came to an end, and the spheres of influence of Great Britain and Russia were definitely mapped out in that region.

Some authorities were therefore of the opinion that the danger of Russian aggression had passed away. The answer to this was that the Pamir Aggrement had brought Russia a great extension of military and political prestige because she had been allowed to advance her frontiers to the Hindu-Koh. Military experts were at loggerheads. Lord Roberts lent his support to the advocates of retention. In 1895 the danger of an attack upon India from the direction of Chitral was infinitesimal.

1. Cambridge History of India, Vol, VI. p. 463

Maharaja Dalip Singh 1838-1893

Early Life

Maharaja Dalip Singh was the youngest son of Maharaja Ranjit Singh and was born to Maharani Jindan or Jind Kaur, the youngest wife of Maharaja Ranjit Singh. He was born in 1873. Maharani was the daughter of one Manna Singh, an Aulakh Jat who hailed from a small village Chachar, in Gujranwala District, now in Pakistan. On the death of Maharaja Sher Singh, Dalip Singh was proclaimed Maharaja in September, 1843 and the British Government recognised him as the Maharaja of the Panjab with Hira Singh Dogra as his Chief Minister, Sardar Chattar Singh Attariwala's daughter was engaged to Maharaja Dalip Singh.[1]

The Panjab lost her independence on 29th March, 1849[2] as the result of the British victory over the Sikhs in the Second Anglo-Sikh War. A proclamation was made declaring the kingdom of the Sikhs at an end. Maharaja Dalip Singh handed over the famous Koh-i-Noor diamond and stepped down from his illustrious father's throne-never to sit on it again, according to the Second Treaty of Lahore.

Removed from the Panjab

By Lord Dalhousie's orders Maharaja Dalip Singh was removed from the Panjab. Having convinced himself that the Sikh nation was to be subverted, Dalhousie maintained that he could not permit himself to be turned aside from fulfilling the duty which he owed to the security and prosperity of millions of British subjects "by a feeling of misplaced and mistimed compassion for the fate of a child.[3]" In February, 1850 Maharaja Dalip Singh was removed from Lahore to the Fort of Fatehgarh. This fort was built by Nawab Muhammad Khan about 1714 A. D. in Farrakhabad District in the United Provinces. It had passed on to the hands of the British Government in 1802, when it had become the head-quarters of an Agent to the Governor-General[4]

1. The Panjab on the Eve of First Sikh War-H.R. Gupta, p. 29.
   A History of the Sikhs, Vol, II-Khushwant Singh, p. 72
2. A History of the Sikhs, Vol. II-Khushwant Singh, p. 82
3. The Marquess of Dalhousie-W.W. Hunter p. .82
4. The Imperial Gazetteer of India Vol-XII pp. 74-75

Maharaja Dalip Singh lived there till 1854. In 1853 he was converted to Christianty by Dr. (afterwards Sir John) Login, who was the superintendent of his establishment at Fatehgarh.

Removed to England

In March 1854 Dalip Singh left India for England. After some time the estate of Hatherop in Gloucestershire was purchased for him by the India Office at the cost of £185,000. The entire amount invested was debited to the Maharaja's account, However, Dalip Singh found the estate unsuitable. Then with the consent of the Government, which made an advance of £110,000, Dalip Singh purchased the Estate of Elvedon in Suffolk, which he held till his death. The above two deals brought the Maharaja under a heavy debt, which was subsequently the cause of his great financial worries.[1]

Came to India

In 1860 he came to India and stayed at Spence's Hotel in Calcutta waiting for his mother Rani Jindan to come from Nepal, join him and proceed to England. He had great affection for his mother and was never satisfied, till he persuaded her to live with him in England. At this time he was "anxious to go up country and poase in the Panjab as the exiled monarch returned for a space to gladden the eyes of his bereaved people; but Lord Canning had no wish for more rebellion than he had already suppressed. So the triumphal progress was prohibited, and the Maharaja proceeded no further than Calcutta.[2]

Death of Maharani Jindan

"Having became nearly blind, broken in heart and subdued in spirit, Maharani Jindan died in England in 1863 and found her last rest ing place in a London suburb.[3]" Dalip Singh took his mother's rema ins to India and immersed them into the sacred river, the Narbada.

Marriage

On his way back to England, he met in Egypt, a German lady, the daughter of a merchant Bomba Muller in Alexandaria. He married

---

1. Lady Login's Recollections, pp. 208-214
2. Lady Login's Recollections, pp. 207-208
3. History of the Panjab, Muhammad Latif, p, 574

her and had five children, two sons and three daughters. Maharani Bomba, died in 1887 and after that he married an English lady, Ada Douglas Wetherill by name, who survived the Maharaja.

As a Christian

In the earlier years of his stay abroad the Maharaja seems to be loyal to Her Majesty the Queen Victoria and enthusiastic about his new faith. Anyhow, that was the impression on gets from his remarks to Dr. Leitner in 1869 that he was prepared to subscribe a thousand rupees annually to the Panjab University (then under contemplation, "provided the Bible was taught in it. In order to spread the gospel among his benighted fellow countrymen."[1] During this period he is said to be the picture of an English country-gentleman, interested in game and sport.

Financial Difficulties

Gradually, a sense of disillusionment began to get over him, what gave the start to the process was his financial difficulties. His allowance was first fixed at £12,000 per annum. It was increased to £15,000 in 1856 when he was 18 years old. Later on in 1862 it was raised to £25,000. Still, it was insufficient. The extravagant habits of the Maharaja were blamed for this by the India office. Dalip Singh lived beyond his means and ran into debt," according to Khushwant Singh.[2] From the very beginning, his estates were encumbered by the enormous sums lent by the Government for their purchase. They had to be reimbursed and every year a good slice of the Maharaja's allowance was taken away in part payment of the advances plus the heavy interest on them.

Ill Treated

The financial condition of the Maharaja reached a crisis in 1880 when they were thoroughly examined by the government and to pay off his debts further sums were advanced on the condition that the estates would not be considered hereditary, but would be sold at his death.

---

1. Asiatic Qarterly, 1894 Article-L. Griffin
2. A History of the Sikhs, Vol. II-Khushwaut Singh, p. 57n.

This was greatly resented by Maharaja Dalip Singh. He consulted lawyers as to the possibility of filing a suit against the Government. Soon after, a book of grievances was printed. He claimed that he had not been treated fairly in the matter of the annual pension. He was paid much less than what was promised to him by the treaty of 1849. He challenged the interpretation put upon it by the India office as being contrary to the one in which he had been brought up, and he demanded arbitration on this question. He tried to reclaim his kingdom through an appeal. When it failed to interest European powers in helping him to recapture his kingdom[1]. He wanted all the lapses on the deaths of his pensioner relatives and servants should be credited to him. Further, he wanted that his pension should be treated as hereditary. The Government rejected all his claims and requests outright. He then raked up the issue of inheritence of the personal private property of his father.

Here too, he met with little success. His continued disappointment with India office led him to question the very validity of the Second Treaty of Lahore, 1849. It was declared by him and his advisers to be "a high-handed act of power, exercised for the exclusive benefit of the stronger party against the weaker, without any justification from any treaty or right created by international law." The Maharaja's view of the treaty was regarded as valid by the Logins and many others, but it was no better than mere outpouring of a disgruntled mind to the India Office who dismissed the whole thing with an arrogant sneer. In the words of Mr. L. Griffin, "the Government's contention was legal, but ungenerous and short-sighted." so that "naturally Dalip Singh was dissatisfied." The India Office stood condemned by its "unsympathetic attitude" towards him[2].

Ill Treatment made him a Patriot

The difficulties and hardships of the Maharaja turned him into a patriot He thought of his country and fellow-country-men and felt pained over the long distance that separated him from them. He began to brood over his county's ills, besides his own, and was prepared to throw off his allegiance to England and make common cause

1. A History of the Sikhs, Vol. II-Khushwant Singh-p. 87n.
2. Asiatic Quarterly, 1894-L. Griffin.

with her enemies, to renounce Christianity and to appeal to the Sikhs as their leader and Maharaja. "His Majesty Dalip Singh was after this openly talked of at the Northbrook Club with the same spirit as that in which Jacobites used to toast the pretender over the water," writes[1] Griffin. Dr. Leitner took a serious view of it and in 1884,, reprimanded certain Panjabi students who would call on "His Majesty the Maharája Dalip Singh" instead of studying and who joined a meeting at an India Club at which it was announced that he would invade the Panjab next year with a Russian Army[2]."

Renounced Christain Faith

Maharaja Dalip Singh heartily renounced his Christian faith and was utterly against the British government. Lady Login expressed his mental state as under : "I detected fresh evidence of mental and moral deterioration; for his mind, from brooding over on a sense of unjust usage, gradually lost its balance, and he became on easy prey to mischief-mongers, eager to seize an opening to embrass the English government." On August 23rd, 1884, he announced his departure for India, as he could not otherwise undergo all the rites of re-initiaion as a Sikh. The letter was that of one quite 'off his head', and he concluded by bestowing on me his blessing, as "eleventh future Gooroo."

The Maharaja, Lady Login continued, had some what prepared me for this a fortnight previously, when he informed me that 'a great storm was gathering in-India, and he trusted to render such services as would compel the British nation to recognize his claims.' His mother (Maharani Jindan) had told him of a prophecy that he was to return to India to teach the Sikhs. This country (England) was going to the dogs.' It was sad to contemplate such a great empire going to pieces."[3]

From England he was coming to India in 1886 to undergo the rites of reinitiation as a Sikh but was detained by the British at Aden. He, however, fulfilled his wish of rejoining Sikhism. Arrangements were made at Aden for the Sikh ceremony of 'Pahul, Before

1 Asiatic Quarterly-1894-L. Griffin.

2. Asiatic Quarterly-1894-L. Griffin.

3. Lady Login's Recollection-pp. 256-257

this formal conversion, Maharaja Dalip Singh had written a letter to one of his relatives in the Panjab which is quoted below :—

ELVEDEN HALL
THETFORD
SUFFOLK

My dear Sardar Sant Singh,

I am very pleased to receive your letter. I thank you very much for offering me your kind services but there is nothing that I require. As the British Government refuse to do me justice, therefore, I shall leave England on the 16th of December next and take up my residence quietly at Delhi for I am poor now.

I am very pleased to find in you a relative of my dear late mother.

As you are aware by this time that I have rejoined the faith, of my ancestors, I salute you with Gooroojee dee Futteh and remain,[1]

Your affectionate relative,
Dalip Singh

Oct. 7th, 1885

In his new patriotic zeal, Dalip Singh felt ashamed of his having foolishly foresaken the religious creed of ancestors. Finally in 1884 he decided to shift over to Sikhism. In that year he got a family priest from India to teach him the Sikh faith and wrote a letter to a Parsi friend of his, Manockjee Cursetjee, to inform him about "his change of creed from Christianity to Sikhism for the reason that Christianity was the religion of robbers and Plunderers and violators of solemn engagements.[2]"

Maharaja's Movements Watched

At last in 1886 the Maharaja determined to go himself to India and set himself at the head of his faithful subjects. His declared object in so doing was to undergo the rites of reinitiation as a Sikh. Writing on the 7th October, 1885 to his relative Sant Singh as already stated he made it clear that he wanted to leave England, as the British Government had refused to do him justice and wished to take up his

1. Heritage of the Sikhs-Harbans Singh, p. 139
2. Lady Login's Recollection, pp. 256-260

residence quietly at Delhi, for he was poor then. But the Government knew him better. When consulted on the matter, Mr. Griffin advised the Secretary of State against allowing him to leave England. He told him that "Dalip Singh was ready for any mischief and that it was inexpedient to allow him to leave England : that the Sikhs did not care two straws about him, but they were an excitable race ; that no one could calculate what might be the force of national sentiment and that only mad men took lighted candle into powder magazines.[1]"

The Secretary of State was unable to accept this advice, because under the law of England Dalip Singh could not be prevented from leaving the country. However, he was confident that in the event of any unfavourable repercussions in India, the Maharaja could be prevented by the Government of India, from entering India or any part thereof.

The Maharaja's Revolt

Outraged in his tenderest point, and furious at the insult put on him, the Maharaja threw in the face of the Government the pension he had hitherto drawn, left his wife and family in their hands to support, abjured his allegiance, and announced his intention of offering his sword and his services to the Emperors of Russia.

From that moment the European journals were filled with bombastic proclamations on his part, and accounts of interviews he vouchsafed to numerous reporters, each fresh manifesto only doing his cause still greater harm in, the eyes of the. British public.

Reaches Aden and Detained

Dalip Singh reached Aden on the way home in April 1886. Here he was detained, because there was already some commotion in the Panjab raised by the tidings of his return to the motherland. In this situation the loyalist Sikhs, Chiefs, Singh Sabhaites and many others found a much-sought-after opportunity to prove their fidelity to the Government once again. The official action was promptly endorsed. Rather, they offered their support in advance, saying that the return

1. Asiatic Quarterly, 1894

of the Maharaja to India would be a source of great danger and needed to be stopped forthwith. So far as the Maharaja's restricted object of getting the Sikh Pahul (baptism) was concerned, he had his wish fulfilled, for the necessary arrangements for the ceremony were made at Aden. The Maharaja stayed for some time there, but unfortunately fell ill and suffered a serious setback in health.

An Open Revolt of the Maharaja

The Maharaja left Aden for Marseilles on 3rd June 1886. The recent action of the Government had accentuated his hostility to the British. He "vowed an implacable hatred to the Viceroys, Governors, Ministers and High Dignitaries of India and England[1]." A clear indication of this was provided in the following telegram which appeared in the Times of July 5, 1886[2].

> "The Maharaja Dhuleep Singh has written an extraordinary letter to the Times of India. He begins by saying that before quitting England the India Government offered him £50,000[3], provided that he promised never to return to India. He declined adding that he would not accept £500,000. His health having broken down owing to his residence at aden, he is going back to drink the German waters. But although prevented from reaching Bombay, he goes on to say, other roads remain. When he returns, he can land at Goa or Pondicherry or enter the Panjab through Russia".
>
> "In the latter event he supposes that the whole Indian army would be sent to resist him. The Indian taxpayers, he added, will be glad to hear that he has resigned the miserable stipend paid under the iniquitous treaty of annexation. When restored to health he hopes to appeal for pecuniary aid to the oriental liberality of his brother Princes and of the people of India. If, however this Government should

1. Asiatic Quarterly, 1894
2. Asiatic Quarterly, 1894
3. According to Lady Login, the offer was made by the Secretary to State through Col. Sir Owen Burne, It was a sort of hush money, at best a consolation prize, (Lady Login's Recollections, p. 257)

veto their generous impulses, he will transfer his allegiance to some other European Power, which will doubtless provide him with maintenance."

Approached to the French, German & Russian Governments For Help

After spending some months in France he went to Germany and from there to Russia where he was accorded a "benevolent reception." The Russians were not unfamiliar with Maharaja's name. As a matter of fact, they hed been regretting all the time that "he was such a good Christian, as he was thereby utterly lost to the Russian objects among the Sikhs." We have it on record that when the Maharaja was at the Straburg railway Station in 1876, a party of Russian Officers rush ed in eagerly discussing Indian affairs and would have contacted the Maharaja but for the presence there of Dr. Leitner.

Some time after his arrival in Russia, Dalip Singh issued a proclamation, which appeared later on the Times of August 5, 1889. The proclamation denounced by his opponents as the seditious proclamation" is realy a monument of his patriotism. The Times summary of it was as follows :—

> "An appeal by the Maharaja Dhuleep Singh of an extraordinary character, addressed to the natives of India, is published in the Press. In provision of the future and as his Royal decree he demands a monthly subscription of one pice from each of the 250,000,000 but from each in the Panjab one anna. The public debt of India is (in this document) repudiated; the payment of taxes is forbidden, cow-killing is prohibited, prisoners are to be released, and all persons who have suffered tyranny and injustice, caused by the British Government, are to be reinstated in their rights. He proposes entering India with the European army with the material support of Russia.[1]" The appeal of the Maharaja failed to evoke any favourable response from the Sikhs, much less from others. Dalip Singh stayed in Russia till November 1888 and continued his efforts for the Russian aid. But the prospects of success retreated farther and farther away. "As was expected, the Czar treated him

1. History of Panjab-Muhammad Latif, p. 628

coldly, and the Maharaja finding his pretentions of no avail, and seeing that he was no welcome guest at Sir. Petersburg, though in his best policy profess repentance to the Queen."

He never wholly recovered from this shock of the so-called Khalsa Panth's disclaimer. Moreover, the Russian eagerness to help him was seriously affected by the refusal of the Sikh leadership to help him. In great disappointment the Maharaja left Russia for Paris. Soon after he had onattack of paralysis, which compelled him to spend the remaider of his life in France. He died on 22nd October 1893 at the Hotel de la Tremouville (Paris).

Conclusion

Whatever might be the circumstances of the time, it is certain that the arrival of Maharaja Dalip Singh was eagerly awaited particularly by the Sikhs and generally by the Panjabis. The Sikhs had not yet forgotten their good old days and the betrayal of the British Government. About the popular patriotic stir among the people of the Panjab has thus been described by one of his contemporaries like Lieutenant-Governor Sir Michael O'Dwyer : The ex-Maharaja Dalip Singh, who had lived in England as an honoured guest on a generous allowance since 1849, had resented the refusal of the British Government to go on paying his debts, had made a bold attempt to return to India, and when headed off at Aden had found a temporary asylum in Russia, which, since the Panjdeh aggression of March, 1885, had been very hostile to us. The news of the possible return of the son of "the Lion of the Panjab," had revived the national feeling of some of the older Sikhs. I remember near Chunian in Lahore, a gruff old Sikh asking Clark, almost insolently, whether we were going to give back his own to the Ex-Maharaja. A sharp rebuke from Clark and a hint that wild talk of this kind would soon land the Sirkar would stand no nonsense, and the agitation was still-born.[1]"

However, for the general observation of the readers it seems feasible to produce correspondence issued by the Times, August, 31, 1882, where the matter under reference has been dealt in detail.

1. India as I knew it-O'Dwyer, p. 34

7

Panjab During 1892-1902

(Sir Dennis Fitzpatrick 1892-1897)

Life Sketch

Sir Dennis Fitzpatrick, Indian Civil Servant, was born on 26th August, 1887 in Dublin. He was the second son of Thomas Fitzpatrick M.D. of Dublin. He passed the open examination for the Indian Civil Service in 1858 and was posted in the following year to the Panjab as Assistant Magistrate at Delhi. He established legal reputation over the case of Begum Samru of Sardhana 1866-72 which was still further enhanced by his tenure of the office of Deputy Secretary from 1874-1876 and Secretary from 1876 to 1877. He remained Chief Commissioner of Central Provinces and member of Royal Commission on the Public Services in 1887. He acted as Resident in Mysore and Chief Commissioner of Coorg and Assam and was promoted as Resident at Hyderabad in 1889.

Fitzpatrick received the C.S.I. in 1887, was Knighted K.C.S.I. in 1890 and in 1892 returned to the Panjab as Lieutenant Governor. In general he devoted his intention to improving the standard of routine efficiency rather than to the new departures. His salutary influence was lessened, however, by his habit of recording his orders, as well as the reasons for them, at the utmost length. Yet he inspired complete confidence and enjoyed universal loyalty and affection; and efficiency of his Govt. He was proved by its successful handling of famine conditions without recourse to a proclamation of famine. He retired in 1897 and was immediately appointed to the Council of India, of which in 1901 he became Vice-President. In 1911 he was promoted G.C.S.I. He died in London on 20th February 1920.

Sir William Macworth Young 1897-1902 Life Sketch

Sir William Macworth Young, was the third son of Captain Sir George Young Second Baronet. of Formosa Place, Cookham, Barkshire, was born at Cookham on 15th August, 1840. He was educated at Eton and Kings College Cambridge.

Sir William Macworth Young passed the examination for the Indian Civil Service in 1862, and was posted to the Panjab, where he took up his first appointment in December, 1863. In 1878 he acted as Superintendent of the Kapurthala State and two years later he became Secretary to the Panjab Government, a post which he held for seven years and in which he made his mark. After occupying administrative positions as Commissioner and Financial Commissioner, he was chosen in October, 1893 to be President of a Commission appointed to enquire into the consumption and control of hemp drugs in India. Two years later in 1895 he was made Resident at Mysore, and in 1897 he was appointed Lieutenant-Governor of the Panjab, being created K. C. S. I. in the following June.

The general characteristics of the rule were the steady development of the province, the efficiency of the steps taken to meet occurrences of famine, and the maintenance of good relations with the people. "In the spring of 1897, Sir Fitzpatrick was succeeded by Sir Macworth Young who had served in almost every executive administrative, and secretariat office, and had also such experience of the Government of India and of the political Department. He was a man of charming personality and acute intellect; but as he said when he laid down his office five years later, he spared none of the great calamities, war, famine and pestilence which scourge a people. The Frontier from Chitral to Waziristan was in a blaze from May, 1897 to 1898, and one result of the conflagration was the bitter controversy over the capacity of the Panjab Government to administer the Frontier districts and the relations of the Frontier tribes on our side of the Dur and Line. The unshot was the decision of Lord Curzon's Government in 1901 to separate these areas from the Panjab, and from them into a separate administration under a Chief Commissioner at Peshawar, directly under the Government of India."[1]

In 1900 Lord Curzon had taken up the question of the administration of the North-West Frontier which was at that time under

1. India as I knew it-O'Dwyer, p. 89

the control of the Panjab Government. In December of that year the Secretary of State approved his proposal to remove the Frontier Districts from the Panjab Government, and place them directly under the Government of India. William Young much resented the proposed dismemberment of province with which he had so long been associated. Thus his relations with Viceroy, Lord Curzon, got strained. He retired in 1902. He was the active supporter of missionary work. He died on 10th May, 1924 at Wey-bridge.

During this period the colonization of the vast area of waste Commanded by the Lower Chenab canal was carried out, and the Lower Jhelum Canal was formally opend six months before Sir Macworth Young left. Full account of the Lower Chenab and the Lower Jhelum Canals has separately been discussed. In 1896-99, the Panjab had again suffered from famine and again in 1899-1900 about which mention has already been made.

Plague-1897

Plague was imported from China, which had first shown itself in Bombay in 1896, broke out in epidemic form in the Panjab in the succeeding years, and the drastic measures taken to cope with it caused some local outbreaks and severely tried the resources of the Panjab Government. Macworth Young faced all this with a gallant spirit.

The first outbreak of plague occurred in October, 1897, in a village Khatkal Kalan of Jullundur District, but infection had probably been imported from Hardwar in May, 1896. For these years the disease was almost entirely confined to the adjacent parts of Jullundur and Hoshiarpur Districts but in November, 1900, it broke out in Gurdaspur and soon spread to the neighbouring District of Sialkot. In 1901 outbreaks occurred in severral Districts; since then the disease had spread widely, and the Province had never been completely free from it. The number of deaths was comparatively small till 1901 when 20, 998 were recorded. In 1902, mortality increased more than tenfold, and the epidemic still continued.

Measures Adopted

The deaths from plague in 1905 numbered 390,233 or 15.8 per thousand of population. The usual measures had been adopted for dealing with outbreaks of plague and with the object of preventing its spread, including the isolation of plague patients and the segregation of persons which had been exposed infection, the evacuation of houses and villages, and the disinfection of houses and effects. Medical treatment and anti-plague inoculation had always been freely offered, but the people had usually preferred native medicines, and the attempts which were made to eradicate or diminish plague by means of inculation could not prove successful. Until May, 1901 most of the precautions, with the exception of medical treatment and inoculation, were compulsory ; but since then compulsion was gradually abandoned, and was chiefly restricted to the reporting of plague occurrences, and the inspection or detention of persons, travelling either by road or railway to certain hill stations.[1]

Riot at Garhshankar

Plague entered the Hoshiarpur District from Jullundur in 1897 ; and, in spite of considerable opposition culimnating in a serious riot at Garhshankar, vigorous measures were for three years taken to stamp out the disease, and to some extent successfully.[2]

Huts made by Villagers

Huts were supplied ready made to the villagers by the Government. At first in the villages of Khatkar Kalan, Jhander Khurd and Khan Khanan the plan was adopted by supplying materials to the villagers, and rewards were given for huts made out of those materials and also for huts made entirely by the villagers from their own materials but even in these villages a large number of huts made by Government were distributed.

Of these three villages the best huts were made at Khan Khanan, as were natural from a village so expert in carpentry. At Jhander Khurd and Khatkar Kalan the people used the ordinary 'sirki hut' but strengthened it against rain and wind by stacking maze stalks against the sides ; but these stalks were not at all pleasant when

1. Jullundur District Gazetteer pp. 19-20
Hoshiarpur District Gazetteer p. 31

saturated with rain. At Khan Khanan the people used 'phus' instead, and this made an admirable thatch. The huts at Khan Khanan were more spacious and stronger. Mr. Jones says in his diary of 1st December 1897. The people are now ready to go out and build huts for themselves, although we have no material but string to give them ; and the Jamindars of Patti Dalel Singh began constructing huts with ladders, old sticks and new cut branches. They will thatch and wall them with Indian corn and hemp stalks" The 'phus' was collected by Mr. Jones' orders from the public roads round Banga.[1]

Causes of the disease

Human agency was not the means of infection

At the commencement, when the disease broke out in widely separated villages, there could be no question that human agency was the means of infection. Sufficient evidence was obtained to show that there was no necessity to have recourse to any other theory. Possibly in some cases the disease might have been conveyed in bundles of clothes, but in the great majority of instances it was found that some persons had come from an infected village and brought the disease with him.

Rats Were The Agents of Infection

When, however, in March and April the disease was increasing at such a rapid rate and when it was found that it was not attacking widely distant villages, but was spreading from an infecting centre to all the villages round that centre, and that too in spite of the cordon and without any evidence of infection by human agency, it was held that rats must in many cases have been the infecting agents.

So far as was ascertained, people conveyed the disease from village to village when going about their ordinary pursuits. In some cases men had broken the cordon to go and condole with friends in other villages, or to attend a religious gathering, bringing back from it sometimes food and sometimes clothes. In many cases the persons had not contracted plague themselves, but had given it to members of their household on their return.

---

1. Panjab Administration Report, 1901-1902, pp. 23-25

Ignorance of the people was the main cause

Mr. Gracey remarks : "The custom in this country that the relatives of a sick or dying person should come and sit round him had a lot to do with the spread of plague, and it was particularly important that all the relatives of an infected person should be immediatly traced, and, if necessary, segregated. The family gatherings at marriages was also a means of spreding infection, and cordons broken by many to attend these gatherings. The outbreak at Pharala may have been due to this cause."

Mr. Butler too has brought to light a custom which could have a good deal to do with the spread of the disease. Before plague was known to be in a village, only when people were becoming ill, they got their 'bubos' opened by some 'Chamar' or other women. It was then the custom for the female friends of the patient to come and condole with her, and each one touched the open wound with the edge of her 'chadar'. There could perhaps be no better way of Sprading the disease.[1]

There was a very considerable difference shown in the number of cases occurring in fresh villages before the Ist of May and after it, but the decrease in May could not be attributed to a decrease in virulence, The villages in which the death rate was highest, Garhshankar, Kariha and Garhi were all villages in which the epidemic was raging at the end of April, and in which immediate evacuation was not enforced. The microbe had certainly not lost its power then, and if fresh villages infected after Ist May showell very few cases, the cause could not properly be attributed to any failure in power, since loss in virulence was always gradual, never sudden. Similarly very little was to be gained by any examination of the proportion of deaths to total cases in the May villages as compared with those in the former months. The proportion was very heavy in Laroya, 10 to 13, and light in Pharala, 6 to 17. both infected in May. These proportions did not differ much from those in March and April villages. These did not appear, therefore, to be any good ground for holding that the disease was losing its virulence in May or that the occurrence of so few cases in

1. Report on outbreak of plgaue, 1897-98, Captain James, pp. 21-22.

that month was to be attributed to any other cause than the speed with which infected villages were then evacuated.

A contemporary and all over picture of this menace is given hereunder.

"There are several points in the Report on the Sanitary Administration of the Panjab just issued to which public attention might be called. The year 1905 to which the Report refers was noted for a defective monsoon, and there was subsequently no serious outbreak of malarial fever, cholera or smallpox. But for the plague which has for several years past seriously affected the vital statistics throughout the Province, the year would have been characterised by a fairly clean bill of health. The death rate in the Province stood as high as 47.55 per mile although it is less than what it stood in 1904, viz. 49.06 per mille. We regret to have to observe in this connection that for the fourth year in succession this Province showed the highest ratio of mortality in India. It may also be stated that out of the 956,108 deaths that took place in the Province in 1905, the plague claimed 334,897[1]."

CHITRAL CAMPAIGN

Chitral was a state in the Dir, Swat, and Chitral Agency of the North-West Frontier Province, with an area of about 4,500 square miles. It comprised the whole of Kashkar Bala or Upper Kashkar, i. e. the Tirich valley, which runs northward from Tirich Mir for 60 miles until it joins the Turikho valley ; thence the combined streams run south for 40 miles through the Mulkho valley and join the Kho valley below Mastuj. The Turikho valley lies north-east and south-west parallel with the Yar Khun, and has a length of 60 miles.

In 1885-86 Chitral was visited by the Lockhart mission ; and in 1889, on the establishment of a Political Agency in Gilgit, Aman ul-Mulk received a subsidy from the British Government of Rs. 6,000 per annum. Some rifles were also given to him. In 1891, this subsidy was increased to Rs. 12,000, on condition that he accepted the advice of Government in all matters connected with foreign policy and the defence of the frontier.

1. The Daily Tribune, February 24, 1907

Afzal Mulk Murdered

In 1892, Aman-ul-Mulk died suddely. His second son Afzal Mulk, who happened to be on the spot, seized the throne. The eldest son, Nizamal-Mulk, governor of Yasin fled to Gilgit. Before Afzal Mulk had fairly emba rked on the necessary extirpation of his other half-brothers, Umra Khan of Jandol, who was at this time master of Dir, invaded Chitral territory and seized the fort and district of Narsat. Afzal Mulk was about to march against him when his uncle Sher Afzal, who had been a refugee in Afghanistan, returned suddenly with a small following. Chitral fort was opened to him, and in the confusion that followed Afzal Mulk was murdered. Sher Afzal proclaimed himself Mehtar. Nizamal-Mulk was then allowed to re-enter Chitral from Gilgit. Sher Afzal, belleving him to have British support, fled before him and Nizam Mulk in turn ascended the throne. He was recognized by Government and a Political Agency was established in Chitral.

Nizam-Ul-Mulk Murdered

In January, 1895, Nizam-ul Mulk was murdered at the instigation of his half-brother Amir-ul-Mulk, acting as the tool of Umra-Khan, who was still occupation of Nasrat and had espoused the cause of Sher Afzal. Amir-ul-Mulk seized the fort. Umra Khan crossed the Lawarai pass with an army, giving out that he was conducting a religious war against the infidels, and asking Amir-ul-Mulk to join him. Amir-ul-Mulk was unable or unwilling to comply, and Umra Khan laid siege to Drosh, which he took after about a month's investment.

Meanwhile, the Political Agent at Gilgit had been sent to Chitral to report on the situation. With his escort, which by reinforcements had been brought up to a strength of over 400 men, of whom 300 belonged to the Kashmir Imperial Service troops, he occupied the fort. All appeared well when suddenly Sher Afzal reappeared on the scene. He was supported by Umra Khan, and was shortly joined by the bulk of the ruling class, the Adamzadas, with their adherents, Amir-ul-Mulk made overtures to them and was consequently placed under restraint in the fort, and Shuja-ul-Mulk, a lad of fourteen, his brother, was provisionally recognised as Mehtar.

The garrison of the fort made an ineffective sortie, and were then besieged from March 3 till April 19, 1895. During the continuance of the siege two notable successes were gained elsewhere by the enemy. The first was the treacherous capture at Buni of two British officers, the destruction of their following, and the seizure of 40,000 rounds of ammunition. The two officers were kept as prisoners by Umra Khan at Munda for nearly a month and were then released on the approach of the relief force. The other success was the practical anihiliation near Rashung of a detachment of 100 men of the 14th Sikhs under Captain Ross.

At Chitral, however, the besieged, though in considerable straights, held out gallantly until the approach of a small force from Gilgit caused their assailants to withdraw. A week later (April 26) the advanee guard of the main relief force, which had been despatched via the Malakand and Dir, entered Chitral territory over the Lawarai pass. Sher Afzal was taken prisoner and Umra Khan fled to Afghan territory. Sher Afzal, Amir-ul-Mulk, and their leading followers were deported to India and the selection of Shuja-ul-Mulk as Mehtar was confirmed. Since then Chitral enjoyed an unwanted peace. The British garrison, most of which was stationed at Drosh, was reduced to a single regiment of native infantry, relieved annually by the Swat and Dir route. Hospitals were opened at Chitral, Mastuj, and Drosh. Cultivation was extended and the Mehtar's revenue continued to increase, while at the same time his mental horizon was much enlarged by his visits to Calcutta in 1900, to the Delhi Darbar in 1903, and to Peshawar in 1904.

Mention should here be made of the Chitral levies, 200 strong, who were raised in 1899 for the defence of Lower Chitral. In 1903 the Chitral Scouts were raised, with the Mehtar as honorary commandant. Their object was to provide a wholly irregular force of craftsmen for the defence of the country in case of invasion. The corps had a total strength of 1,200 men, but all of these were never embodied at one time.

TIRAH CAMPAIGN

A mountainous *tract of unadministered territory in the* North

West Frontier Province was inhabited in the summer months by all the sections of the Orakzai, two sections of Jowaki Afridis, and by the Kulla Khel subsection of the Asho Khel sections of the Adam Khel Afridis. The name was also used in an extended sense to include almost the whole territory except the Bazar and Khaiber valleys inhabited by those tribes, the portions occupied by them in the winter months being distinguished as Lower Tirah.

Tirah thus consists of the country watered by the Mastura, one of the main branches of the Bara, which flows through the centre of the country, the Khanki Toi, and the Khurmana-three rivers which rise within a few miles of Mittughar (12, 470 feet), a point on the Safedkoh.

The original inhabitants of Tirah were the Tirahis, probably a Tajik race, who were driven out of the country by the Pir-i-Roshan[1] and a remnant of them fled to Nangrahar.

Since the decay of the Mughal empire Tirah had been virtually independent, though owning at times a nominal allegiance to Kabul. Tirah was first entered by a British force in 1897, when the Orakzai and Afridis rose in 'Jehad' or religious war against the British. The Orakzai attacked the Samana, and the Afridis attacked Landi Kotal and the other posts in the Khaiber Pass. These violations of British territory necessitated the dispatch of 34,500 men into Tirah, under Sir William Lockhart. The main body advanced from Shinawari in the Miranzai valley over the Chagur Kotal, and precipitous heights of Dargai near which, being held in force by the enemy. were gallantly stormed. The troops advanced across the Khanki and Mastura valleys over the Sampagha and Arhanga passes to Maiden and Bazar, whence the whole of Tirah was overrun returning to Peshawar by the Bara valley in December.

WAZIRISTAN CAMPAIGN

Waziristan was a Political Agency in the North-west Frontier Province, with an area of about 2, 310 square miles. It was bounded on the north and east by the Districts of Kohat and Bannu, and on the south by the Khaktu stream, from the point where it entered the

1. The apostle of hight.

latter District to Shuidar at its head. From Shuidar the boundary followed the eastern watershed of the Shwal valley as far as Drenashtar Sar, and then ran northeast along the Durand Line to Kohisar in the country of the Kabul khel wazirs and Biland Khel.

Comprised Four Valleys

The Agency thus comprised four large and fettile valleys : in the north, the Lower Kurram valley between the Kurram Agency on the upper reaches of that river and Bannu district ; the Kaitu valley ; DAUR in the valley of the Tochi, the most open and fertile of the four ; and the Khaisora valley in the south. Between the Kaitu and Tochi lay the Sheratulla and, north of Miram Shah, the Dande two barren plains, each about 30 square miles in area. Another plateau, called the Spereragha similar to the Sheratulla but smaller, lay between the Kurram and the Kaitu.

Valleys were separated by High Barren Hills

With these exceptions, the valleys were separated by high barren hills. The loftiest peak was Shidar (11,000 feet), at the western end of the Khaisora valley. The hills were generally composed of Oceanic sandstone and conglomerate, through which great masses of limestone cropped up, and their surface covered with crumbling soil, which in the flood time filled the streams with the silt that fertilises the valleys. The low-lands were feverish and unhealthy from August to October, and in the summer months the people migrated to Shuidar highlands, which enjoyed a perfect climate. With the exception of the Dàurs of the Daur valley, the people of Northern Waziristan all belonged to the Darwesh Khel branch of the Wazirs, who were divided into two main sections, the Utmanzai and Ahmadzai. Both these sections were subdivided into numerous clans. The Darwesh Khel were the least tractable of the Pathan tribes, and their continued raids on the Daurs impelled the latter in 1894 to petition the British Govrnment for protection.

Daur was taken over

In consequence, Daur was taken over and was put under a form of direct administration, while the wazirs were merely under political control. Under the agreement made with the Amir of Afghanistan in

1893, the boundary of that State was demarcated in 1894-95 without open opposition from the Darwesh Khel. Raids in British territory, however, continued, and in 1897 troops were sent from Datta Khel to enforce the collection of a fine which had been imposed on the village of Maizar. The villagers treacherously attacked the British force, killing five British officers and men, and as a punishment their lands were laid waste by a military expedition. The tribe then submitted, and the Wazirs held aloof from the subsequent risings on the North-West Frontiers, though their raids continued.

For some years the tract between Thal and the Tochi in the Lower Kurram Valley inhabited by the Kabul Khel section of Utmanzai remained a veritable Alsatia, in which a number of out laws from British territory found a refuge. Finally, in November, 1902, columns entered it from the Tochi, Bannu, and Thal. The tribesmen offered but little opposition, but at Gumatti a gang of outlaws made a desperate resistance. All towers were blown up and their rebuilding was not permitted. Large numbers of outlaws (about 250) surrendered themselves after the operations, and the country was since then opened by the tribe to the passage of troops and British officers. Roads were made from Thal to Idak in Tochi and to Bannu. Peace was kept in the Tochi valley, the only portion of the agency which was administered, by a militiary corps of 1,318 men, of whom 106 were mounted.

The Political Agencies

The necessity of improving the relations of the British districts with the trans-border tribes was constantly felt by the British administrators and statesmen since the occupation of the North-west Frontier Province, as a part of the Panjab. A special political agency for the Khaiber was started in 1878, with duty to keep the pass open. The cession of Kurram in 1879 by the Afghan Government, led to a similar agency being created for Kurram area in 1892.

Durand Line

Durand Line decision is equally important to link with the present events of the North-West Frontier Province and the retrospect of it seems necessary to be briefed here. Sher Ali withdrew to

Russian territory, where he died ; and his son Yaqub Khan, agreed to the treaty of Gandmak 1880, by which he was settled as Amir of Kabul as soon as he had agreed to receive a British Resident at Kabul and to cede to the English certain districts of Loralai, Zhob, Pishin, Quetta, and Nushki including the British occupation of the passes. The attempt to put a British envoy at the Afghan Capital, after the first phase of the Second Afghan War in 1879, had ended in a fierce rising against the British Residency, resulting in the murder of the envoy Sir Louis Cavagnari. The boundary line fixed in 1880, added the Eastern half of the old sub-province of Kandhar to the Indian Empire : but the modified Frontier line fixed in 1894 along the top hills of the Suleman range of mountains, and known as the durand line, then brought the tribes-men living in the Khaiber, and Mohmand Tirah, Kurram, and Waziristan, within the British sphere of influence. The position of the British Government in the North-West Frontier districts became stronger when the Eastern slopes of the Suleman mountains came within their control.[1]

The Durand Line demarcation in 1894, under which the Amir of Kabul ceased to exercise any control of the independent tribes of the border, the British Government assumed a responsibility over the tribal territory intervening between the five settled districts of the North-West Frontier Province, and the rugged mountain regions on the border of Afghanistan. The three remaining agencies of Malakand, Tochi, Wana were developed in 1895-1896. The last two agencies were left in charge of the Panjab Government working through its Commissioners. The Malakand agency was placed directly under the Government of India as it dealt with the area admininistered by the British Government through allied and subordinate Chiefs of Swat, Chitral, Dir, and Bajaur. The independent territory of Tirah, Waziristan and the rest for which the British Government had assumed control under treaty rights with the Amir of Afghanistan, was mainly held by the various tribal laws sanctioned by brute force of arms. The British control was confined to various roads driven up the different passes in Khaibar, Kurram, Tochi, and Gomal for defence purposes.[2]

1. The Evolution of N.W.F. Province-Dewan Chand, p. 42
2. The Evolution of N.W.F. Province-Dewan Chand, pp. 68-69

ALIENATION ACT—1900

Early History

The most fruitful of Thorburn's[1] proposals, was the one which aimed at restricting more effectively the transfer of land from agriculturists to money-lenders. It had always been the policy of the Panjab Government to discountenance such transfers. In 1852 the Board of Administration "had issued a circular requiring a land-owner, who wished to sell his land, to offer it, in the first instance, to the whole village community or to some individual co-partner, at a reasonable rate to be fixed by agreement, failing which the revenue officer and three assessors were to determine the fair value."

Sanctioning Authorities

In 1858 the Commissioner's sanction was required for the sale of ancestral or joint property in land in satisfaction of money debts. In 1859 that of the Judicial Commissioner[2] was required. Afterwards the Financial Commissioner[3] became the authority to whom proposals had to be submitted. "Since 1866 no interest in land could be sold in satisfaction of money debts without such sanction."

The first Civil Procedure Code (1859) confirmed the power of the Civil Courts to attach agricultural land in execution of decrees, but this code was not extended to the Panjab until 1866, and the sections relating to the attachment and sale of agricultural land were subject to special modifications in the Panjab."

Land Selling was Discouraged

In practice applications to sell land were discouraged by the Financial Commissioner, who hardly ever granted them the land when it was ancestral and seldom when it was acquired. They were consequently few in number ; and the execution of decrees against

1. It ultimately resulted in the Land Alienation Act of 1900
2. Land of the Five Rivers-Trevaskis p. 293
3. Land of the Five Rivers-Trevaskis, p. 231.

agriculturists was practically confined[1] to execution against the movable property or persons of the debtr or "An active and persevering decree-holder could often bring pressure in these ways on an agriculturist debtor so as to drive him into selling or mortgaging part of his land by private contract. But as the courts of execution were not disposed to press agriculturist debtors too hard, this did not generally succeed. Later amendments of the Civil procedure Code, however, exempting movable necessaries made this method of compulsion more difficult to decree-holders"; but the very difficulty of bringing pressure to bear on debtors in this way led money-lenders to discover a legal technicality by which land could be attachad and temporarily transferred to them. Such temporary transfers tended to become permanent, and in this way the whole system of restrictions devised by the Panjab Government was gradually circumvented.[2]

Increase In Alienations

The result tended to justify the alarmist attitude of Thorburn. Doubtless the position was considerably better than was the case in the North-Western Provinces, where in ten districts taken at randon in 1873, money.lenders held 27 per cent of the total area as against 10 per cent thirty years earlier, and where in one district nearly half the area had changed hands between 1851 to 1881.[3]

Nevertheless in spite of the endeavours made by the Panjab Government to restrict alienation, a very careful enquiry made in 1888 led to the conclusion that there had a large and steady increases in alienations and that 8 per cent of the cultivated area was in the hands of mortgagees. A far more serious state of affairs obtained in individual districts.

In the three eastern tahsils of Ambala, a quarter of the total area changed hands during thirty years, over a half of this to money-lenders.

---

1. In the absence of mortgages with conditions of foreclosure of sale.
2. The Wealth and welfare of the Panjab-Culvert p. 123
   Land Administration Manual-D^o^uie, p. 51
   Selections from papers on Indebtedness and Land Transfer pp. 45-68
3. Memorandum on the Restriction of the Power to Alimate interests in Land, p. 33

"In 1917, when I was on recruiting duty in one of these tahsils a large number of Muhammadan Rajputs who volunteered were rejected as unfit by the regimental officer. The device was then adopted of feeding them up for three months before despatch to the regiment, which then gladly accepted them. In fact these lads were half starved and gladly enlisted to get food and clothing. Yet they were the sons of peasant proprietors cultivating their own land in one of the most fertile tracts of the Province. These peasants had got into debt, and had therefore to endure the sight of seeing fat, sleek, money-lenders carrying off the grain they had forcibly raised and so urgently needed for their underfed children[1]." In the Gujranwala tahsil, a favourite recruiting ground for the native army, in twenty-two years money-lenders had acquired possession of one fifth of the whole cultivated area, consisting for the most part of the very best portions[2].

In considering these statistics it should be borne in mind that the area of land actually transferred by no means exhausted the area in which the proprietors interest was lost virtually beyond recall. The successive stages in process of the peasant's enslavement, were, first debt, then simple hypothecation and unsufructuary mortgage and finally sale. The amount of debt, for which, as the law stood the land was liable, was even then enormous, and much of it of such a nature that it must inevitably passed through the further stages to the final conclusion of sale[3].

Alienation Act

On the 8th June, 1901 the Panjab Alienation of Land Act came into force. It was the result of many year's most careful enquiry and was passed into law amidst gloomy forebodings. The Lieutenant-Governor, Sir Mackworth Young, marshalled the opinions of many eminent revenue officers of the past in support of his own view. He complained that the Act was not due to the initiative of the Panjab Government and indeed went beyond its utmost recommendations and explained that he was refraining from opposition only because 'the best

---

1. Land of the Five Rivers-Trevaskis p. 399 fn
2. Memorandum on the Restriction of Power of Alienation Interests in Land p. 34
3. I lid. p. 48

experience available" of his own officers was in favour of the measure. All sorts of evil seemed to be impending. The value of land would be depreciated, the provisions of the Act would be disregarded or evaded, the money-lender's trade would become impossible and the borro wer would be pinched. In point of fact all these gloomy prognostications proved groundless.

The Act was quietly received, apathy was observable than excitement, no special difficulties were encountered and the new law was soon absorbed into the routine life of the province. Its main provisions were very simple. Sale of agricultural land in execution of a decree was forbidden. Sale of their lands by members of agricultural tribes to others who were not members of these tribes was similarly forbidden ; though sanction may be accorded to such sales in special cases. The Bengal form of mortgage, with a conditional sale clause it rendered illegal and even in the case of old mortgages the conditional sale clause become inoperative. All mortgages of land by agriculturists in favour of non-agriculturists were illegal except such as provided for automatic redemption. To obviate evasion, land could not be leased for a period longer than five years.[1]

Opposed by the Urban Bourgeosie

This improvement had been strengthened by this Alienation Act, and the Rural Co-operative Credit Movement. Both measures had been strongly opposed by the urban bourgeoisie who looked on the peasantry as their natural prey. As a result of this increased prosperity, the peasantry and the landed gentry had developed a spirit of healthy independence, and were demanding that the public revenues which they mainly contributed should be spent more for their benefit, and that they should have an increased share in the public services, of which the urban literati had in the past enjoyed the monopoly.

An Evil System

It was recognised that the evil was largely the result of the system introduced by the British with the best of intentions. They reduced the State's share of the proprietary profits of land in order to bring benefit

1. The Wealth and Welfare of the Panjab, Calvert pp. 265-66

to the landed classes but the fruits of Government's sacrifices were being diverted into the pockets of the money lenders. To a large extent Government was responsible, and Government had to discover a remedy. Inaction, as the Vicercy at the time pointed out, was not an alternative adopting a remedy it would be an evasion of responsibility. Palliativeto or even remedial measures would have been insufficient to meet the gravity of the circumstances the evil had to be prevented. It must not be assumed that the decision to impose restiictions on the power of alienation was arrived at without full consideration of all the interest involved. For 25 years as the Annual Land Revenue Reports amply, testify the subject had received unbroken attention, but it was realised that it would be no light matter to restrict a power which had been deliberately and formally conferred. The old-time cultivator had been recognised as full landed proprietor with all the privileges of a yeoman, and in the desire to prevent him from losing his proprietary status nothing could be contemplated that might be regarded by the people as under-mining that status.[1]

THE REMEDIAL MEASURES

The remedial measures that suggested themselves were some what as follows :-

1. The demand for land-revenue and its collection could be made so elastic as to remove this from the list of causes that led to borrowing; this has since been carried into effect;

2. borrowing might be discouraged by limiting the security with the land owner had to offer or by diminishing the facilities for the recovery of debt;

3. the system of agricultural loans could be extended it was, however, obvious that these could never replace the money lender;

4. the enforcement of inequitable contracts could be refused;

5. the liability of the land and its produce for unsecured money debts could be restricted;

6. the power of sale or mortgage of land could be restricted[2].

---

1. The Wealth and welfare of the Panjab calvert, p. 264.
2. Ibid. p, 264

Criticism

Mr. M.L. Darling[1] made two criticisms of the Act which deserve notice:

1. The first was that the protective effect of the measure weakened the independence of the protected. To this the obvious answer was that there was freedom of sale and mortgage within the notified groups. There was ample scope to develop resisting power. The influence of Hindu law and the joint family system on the alienation of ancestral property had been in force for centuries and no prominent Hindu of any caste was agitating for the abolition of these. Again, as has been pointed out, the number of sales of land always been very small and the total area transferred in a year was always a minute fraction so the protection operated only against a rare temptation.

2. The second criticsims was that the Act widens the gulf between the country and town and so restrained the townsman from taking a practical interest in rural questions. This was clearly based on a misunderstanding. There were several times more of the trading castes living in villages than in towns and even in the town they numberd not more than a quarter of the whole. The person inhabited was the village money-lender and outside Multàn he had practically never showed interest in agricultural development. There was a total area of over five million acres owned by those who were not members of notified agricultural tribes, of which over three million acres were cultivated, but the owners had not taken the numerous opportunities open to them to evince any marked interest in agriculture, beyond planting a few gardens.

Auction Sales free

Besides auction sales in the Panjab colonies were free of all restriction, so that there were more than ample opportunity for the great trading and commercial castes to embark on an agricultural career. If it were otherwise, if these important castes and showed real interest in agriculture and its developement on modern scientific lines, if they put capital into the land and produced from it more than their agricultural neignbours then there could be a strong argument for reconsideration;

1. The Panjab Peasant in Prosperity and Debt.

but although there were thousands of owners of land from these castes only every few had taken a practical and serious interest in the development of their estates. The mere fact that most of these non-agriculturists owners let their land to agriculturists on rent should be proof enough of their own belief as to who was best fitted to cultivate it.

Canal Colonies Excluded

Mr Darling excluded the Panjab Canal Colonies from the operation of the Act; there was much to be said in favour of this as there the land was not ancestral and there was no question of peasants being cheated of their ancient patrimony, but enough was said in this respect to prove the evils of tenancy and to allow capitalists to buy out the then agriculturists holders in the colonies would merely increase the evil. It was not claimed that the absentee capitalist landlord was worse than absentee agriculturists landlord. He was certainly not worse but there was always the tendency for one or more of the agriculturists sons to settle on the grant and cultivate it, while the capitalists sons could never weild the plough or sickle. In order provinces of India. in Oudh for instance, there were large capitalist landlords of the noncultivating castes with every opportunity to evince their interest in their estates in a practical way. But the chief result of their existence was difficult problem of landlord and tenant in which government was always being asked to intervene, while the material for agrarian agitation offered constant opportunity and temptation to the professional malcontent which he too frequently made use of to the disadvantage of everyone and the advantage of none.

INDEX